SIMPLICITY SECRET

How to Reduce Overwhelm and Stress,
Make More Money,
Improve Your Health and Fitness,
and Be Happier

GEORGE CHOY & SARAH CHOY

SIMPLICITY SECRET

Simplicity Secret: How to Reduce Overwhelm and Stress, Make More Money, Improve Your Health and Fitness, and Be Happier

First published in the United Kingdom in February 2024 by
My Castle Property Ltd.
© 2024 George David Choy & Sarah Jane Choy

George David Choy and Sarah Jane Choy have asserted their right to be identified as the authors of this work in accordance with sections 77 and 78 of the Copyright, Designs and Patents Act 1988.

All rights reserved. No part of this book may be reproduced by any means, electronic, mechanical, photocopying or otherwise, without the prior permission of the publisher.

British Library Cataloguing in Publication Data
A catalogue record is available for this book

Paperback ISBN: 9798871104064
Hardback ISBN: 9798879184020

Disclaimer

The information provided in this book and accompanying materials are for general informational purposes only and do not constitute advice. The contents are not tailored to your specific circumstances. The contents of this book and accompanying materials do not constitute investment, financial, tax, accounting, pension, legal, medical, fitness, health, psychological or mental health advice and neither the authors nor interviewees nor My Castle Property Ltd are financial advisors, accountants, tax specialists, debt professionals, pension advisors, solicitors, lawyers, lettings agents, estate agents, building surveyors, mortgage advisors, medical professionals, dietitians, psychiatrists, psychologists or therapists. You must not rely on the information in this book or accompanying materials as an alternative to financial, investment, legal, taxation, accounting, pension, mortgage, psychological, diet, medical or other advice from an appropriately qualified professional. You should never delay seeking professional advice because of the information contained in this book or accompanying materials. Investing in financial markets and alternative investments involves inherent risks, and past performance is not indicative of future results. Performance data, in addition to laws and regulations, change over time, which could change the status of the information in this book. This book and accompanying materials are not intended to serve as the basis for any financial decision or as an offer to sell or purchase any investment or alternative investment. No warranty is made with respect to the accuracy or completeness of the information contained herein or in the accompanying materials, and both the authors, interviewees and My Castle Property Ltd specifically disclaim any responsibility for liability, loss, or risk, personal or otherwise, which is incurred as a consequence, directly or indirectly of the use and application of any of the contents of this book or accompanying materials. This book and accompanying materials and emails may contain links to affiliate websites, and we may receive affiliate commission for any qualifying purchases made by you on the affiliate website using such links. Please assume all links could be affiliate links. This disclaimer will be governed by and construed in accordance with English law, and any disputes relating to this disclaimer will be subject to the exclusive jurisdiction of the courts of England and Wales.

Acknowledgements

Our heart overflows with gratitude for the incredible souls who poured their time and love into the interviews for *Simplicity Secret*.

Your warmth and generosity have left an unforgettable mark and we are truly touched.

Thank you from the bottom of our heart.
Sarah & George Choy xxx
sarahandgeorge.co.uk

With thanks to:

Sarah Beth
Sarah Beth Yoga

Jack Boken
Happy Jack Yoga

Deanna Breiwick
International Opera Singer & Voice Coach

Diana Finch-Keran
Yoga teacher, Essex, UK

Other Books by Sarah & George Choy

Stealth Millionaire:
How to Save and Manage Your Money Like the Rich
https://bit.ly/stealthbook

Find Your Purpose:
A Practical Guide for Discovering Your Purpose and Creating a Life You Love
bit.ly/fypurpose

Contents

CHAPTER 1 11
THE POWER OF SIMPLICITY 11
Introduction 11
Navigating the Storm: Sarah and George's Journey 16

CHAPTER 2 25
FREE BONUS CONTENT 25

CHAPTER 3 27
DEVELOPING YOUR VISION 27
How Are You Feeling Right Now? 27
Creating Three Months of Joy 27
Envisioning a Simplified and Fulfilling Life 29
The Science of Manifesting Your Dream Life 30
CREATING YOUR SIMPLICITY PLAN 32
Domino Action Plan 32
Limit Your Projects 36

CHAPTER 4 37
UNLOCKING THE SIMPLICITY SECRET 37
Dissatisfiers 37
Simplicity Secret Tool 39
Decision Fatigue Results In Crap Decisions 44

CHAPTER 5 47
MAKE MORE MONEY 47
Mastering the Art of Saving: Your Path to Financial Freedom 49
Conquering Debts: The Road to Liberation 52
Conquering Expenses for a Richer Tomorrow 55
Living a Richer Life 61
From Savings to Fortune: The Art of Growing Your Wealth 63
Stress-free Retirement 70
Advanced Planning: If I Die 72

Interview: Diana Finch-Keran, UK Yoga Teacher............. 73
Conclusion: Money.. 77

CHAPTER 6 79
ENJOY YOUR WORK AND MISSION 79
Are you in the right job? 80
You're getting paid even less than you think!.............. 84
Getting Shit Done!... 85
Making Business Simple 95
Interview: Sarah Beth, Sarah Beth Yoga 107
Conclusion: Work and Mission 123

CHAPTER 7 125
NURTURING HEALTHY RELATIONSHIPS 125
Surround Yourself With Greatness 127
Letting Go of Toxic Relationships 129
Communication Strategies for Relationship Simplicity 129
Balancing Personal and Professional Connections........... 131
Interview: Deanna Breiwick, International Opera Singer & Voice Coach 132
Conclusion: Relationships 137

CHAPTER 8 139
FROM CHAOS TO CALM: BRING SIMPLICITY AND ORDER TO YOUR HOME 139
Decluttering Your Home for Mental Focus and Emotional Well-being 140
How Large a Home Do You Need? 143
Fix Dissatisfiers in Your Home 143
Habitualising Weekly Routines 144
The Magic of Lists 145
Separating Work and Home Life................................. 145
Striking a Balance with Technology............................ 146
Interview: Jack Boken, Happy Jack Yoga 148
Conclusion: Home Life 151

CHAPTER 9 153
SIMPLIFY HEALTH AND FITNESS 153

Introduction **153**
Simplifying Your Diet for a Long Life **156**
Monitoring Your Health **174**
Habitualise Your Fitness Routine **176**
Burn Fat in Your Sleep **181**
Conclusion: Health and Fitness **183**

CHAPTER 10 .... **185**
TOOLS TO REDUCE OVERWHELM AND STRESS 185
Introduction **185**
Embrace Daily Nurturing **186**
Express Your Feelings **187**
Hug It Out **188**
Meditation—the Stress Buffer **188**
One Mindful Breath **191**
Letting Go of Suffering **192**
Yogic Breathwork **193**
Gaming Therapy **194**
What if… **194**
Conclusion: Stress Relieving Tools **196**

CHAPTER 11 .... **197**
AND THEN WHAT? FINDING FULFILMENT 197
Love and Connection **197**
Growth **198**
Contribution **198**
Spirituality **198**
Conclusion: Finding Fulfilment **199**
Thank You for Your Service **200**

REFERENCES **204**

CHAPTER 1

The Power of Simplicity

"You have to work hard to get your thinking clean to make it simple. But it's worth it in the end because once you get there, you can move mountains."
— Steve Jobs, co-founder Apple Inc.

INTRODUCTION

Simplicity Secret will help you whenever you feel overwhelmed or stressed—and create a solid foundation for a life of joy and fulfilment. You'll also learn the stress-busting tools that will give you instant relief. Not only that, but we'll show you the simple ways to become more successful in your life by doing less.

In addition, **you'll be treated to inspiring interviews** with individuals who've harnessed the power of simplicity, **including Sarah Beth Yoga, Happy Jack Yoga, Deanna Breiwick, and Diana Finch-Keran.**

My wife Sarah and I found ourselves staring at a tsunami of stress. Wave after wave of stressful events crashed upon us, creating a relentless pile-up in our money, work, relationship, kids and home life.

Just when we believed the storm couldn't intensify any further, we were both diagnosed with medical problems.

It felt like we were caught in a hurricane. This turbulent sea of stress paralyzed us, magnifying even the simplest irritations, as our capacity to cope with life crashed into the rocks. I just wanted to curl up into a ball and hide in a cave.

Yet, amid the chaos, we discovered a glimmer of hope, a lifeboat to escape the suffocating grip of our complicated existence—simplicity.

In the next sub-chapter, we'll bare all, sharing with you the overwhelming events we experienced—and how we got through it.

It's not surprising that we're all stressed. Welcome to the chaos of modern life. In the relentless pursuit of accomplishments, society has convinced us that juggling more tasks than a caffeinated octopus is the key to success!

We've all mastered the art of multitasking to the point where we listen to podcasts while walking, driving, and probably even in our sleep. We work on our laptops on trains and planes, check email and social media while standing in queues, and go on conference calls while "relaxing" on one of our two planned vacations for the year. Absolutely. Bring on the multitasking frenzy!

Weekends? What are they? Those are just extra hours for us to reply to emails, texts and social media notifications—and somehow look after our family in-between. Hitting those endless phone notifications is like being in an eternal game of Whac-A-Mole.

It's no wonder that in the endless pursuit of doing more, we find ourselves ensnared in a web of stress and anxiety. Stress is the permanently annoying background noise to our daily symphony of chaos.

The pressure to keep up, the fear of not being good enough, and the constant feeling that you haven't done enough—these are the ingredients for feeling overwhelmed. They drown out what should be our natural melody of contentment, joy, and bliss. There's a growing community of people yearning for a less demanding, simpler life.

It comes as no surprise that research commissioned by the UK's National Health Service found that 1 in 6 people will experience a mental health problem such as anxiety or depression, in any given week.[1]

> *"Most people mistake movement for achievement."*
> *— Tony Robbins*

And although we're keeping endlessly busy, are we really focusing on the most important things?

When life feels like a hamster wheel on steroids, and you're overwhelmed and on the brink of shutting down like a startled rabbit—that's when you start thinking, "Maybe simplicity is the way to go." It is often only when we've reached overwhelming pain that we seek a simpler life.

In Simplicity Secret, you'll discover the art of reducing complexity, minimizing moving parts, and regaining control over your life. Taking the simple path is often the quickest way to achieve your goals.

> *"Complexity is the enemy of execution."*
> —Tony Robbins

Simplicity isn't a sacrifice—it's an investment in a life of purpose and joy. From the seemingly mundane tasks of your daily routine to the intricate dance of your relationships, simplicity is the guiding principle that can transform the ordinary into the extraordinary.

Join us on this thing called life, as we unveil the *Simplicity Secret Tool*—your ticket to a life less stressed and a feeling of peace and happiness.

We want to create the best book ever for you, so by utilising the Simplicity Secret tool, **we'll delve into simplifying the five areas of your life and share the top strategies that actually work when it comes to:**

1. Money
2. Work and Mission
3. Relationships
4. Home Life
5. Health and Fitness

…proving that simplicity isn't just a philosophy—it's a roadmap to a richer life.

And remember, sometimes the solution is as simple as deciding to take the next step. So, face the storm, take the plunge, and let's turn those dreams into your reality!

As well as conquering the five areas of life, we'll give you tools to overcome overwhelm and stress. Then we'll sprinkle in some suggestions to spice up your happiness and bring you fulfilment. It's time to rewrite the success script. It's not about doing a million things or living in a cave—it's about the quality and richness of your life.

Your past does not dictate your future.

Grab the steering wheel and cruise towards to your destiny.

The route to a stress-free existence awaits you.

You've got the power within you, and it's time to unlock the *Simplicity Secret* **and set your life ablaze!**

Navigating the Storm: Sarah and George's Journey

My wife Sarah and I used to thrive on being constantly busy. Even after reaching a point where we didn't need to work anymore, our long to-do list was filled with big projects unfolding simultaneously.

When life gets tough, and shit hits the fan, it's often during your darkest moments that you make profound realisations and significant transformations.

It all began during a period of huge expansion across our businesses.

The initial crack in our home life appeared when our daughter started encountering difficulties in school. Overwhelmed by anxiety and constant worry, she became more and more difficult to motivate to go to school. She was 11, but it got to the point where she was having **90-minute tantrums in the morning**, and Sarah ended up driving her late to school, and leaving her at the reception desk in tears. It was awful.

Her behaviour at home was very difficult, and we ended up taking her out of school, as she refused to go at all. After a month though, it was clear that she was not going to learn at home with Sarah, so we arranged to send her back to school.

This time she was placed in a specialized small class, designed to support children with similar struggles. Unfortunately, while there were benefits of being in a smaller class, mixing with emotionally fragile kids lead her to a **turbulent rollercoaster of emotions**, and a lot of class disruption. She often felt she had no friends and was worthless. Sarah was not convinced she was learning much, as the teachers spent a lot of time managing the behaviour of the other students.

In our training business, we'd just finished a month of launching our latest training course. We knew our programs were really helpful to people, but the level of energy required to sell them was draining. We are not particularly natural salespeople. But as it was just the two of us in the company, we had to do it anyway, in order to share our knowledge and skills. **I was left feeling so exhausted, that I just wanted to curl up into a ball and live in a cave.** The idea of another launch in three months-time felt overwhelming.

We were committed to hosting multiple mentoring calls every week. **While we enjoyed helping people, we had overcommitted ourselves.** We even took calls during our vacations, and only took one week off from calls in the entire year—for Christmas. We put on a brave face during the calls, but deep down we were feeling burned out and struggling.

Then the hints of a larger storm began, with trouble **attempting to simultaneously refinance four residential properties, with a single mortgage company.** The lender was playing hard to get and kept asking for more and more paperwork. We'd never experienced difficulties like this in the past. **We got the overall feeling that they didn't want to lend right now.** The Bank of England base rate had been static at 0.1% for the last two years, and it suddenly jumped to 0.75% over 3 months—it looked as though the rates would skyrocket (and they did). The mortgage lenders were feeling really uncertain about what interest rates to charge and were pulling mortgage products off the market every day. The whole economy seemed to be teetering on the edge.

The mortgage company said they would only provide mortgages if we did such and such—which we did with great pains…then they'd come up with something else…and something else after that. **We felt like we were pushing water uphill.**

This dragged on for another four months, by which time the bank base rate had increased by another 1% due to high inflation. The financial markets were being given the expectation that the interest rate would likely increase another 4-5% over the next year or more. It got to the point where **I think the lender had zero interest in processing our mortgage**, because they would be losing money on the offer they'd sent us at the beginning.

Meanwhile, we were trying to mortgage a commercial property we owned outright. It felt like déjà vu with the lender showing reluctance—making it another uphill battle. Trying to execute our plans was proving tougher than expected. With substantial sums of money at stake, it added an extra layer of stress.

Adding to the already overwhelming situation, **one of our commercial properties was experiencing a severe roof leak**, with water cascading through the ceiling courtesy of the relentless weather. The tenant resorted to placing buckets strategically to catch the downpour. Unfortunately, finding a qualified roofer for repairs three-stories high was a challenge in itself. We managed to secure one, but the repairs stretched for months, unveiling a cascade of leaks, one after another. Understandably, the tenant flooded us with a barrage of irate emails.

We had recently completed the purchase of a warehouse and were in the process of agreeing a lease for a new tenant. We were excited to add another commercial property to our portfolio, but it was a new build and the legals had been tricky. The warehouse had only recently been split from the other units in the industrial estate, so getting individual searches and utilities was time consuming. We had used a commercial agent to find us a tenant. They found an established firm, but this was their first project in the UK, as they were European. Agreeing terms with the tenant in a second language and getting them moved in took some energy, as everything in England was new to them.

We were also going through legals to buy an agricultural property—which we intended to get planning permission on and build our new home. We had not specifically been looking for one but had switched on Rightmove Commercial alerts out of habit. Interestingly, Sarah and I had both seen the property listing, thought it was very interesting, and not mentioned it to the other! It came up in conversation, and we explored it further, running some numbers and talked it through with our property mentors. We all thought it seemed interesting, and potentially lucrative over the long term.

We had planned on building our own home for many years and had been on the local self-build council register without any success. We'd bid on other plots without getting them. This one seemed viable, so we put in a bid and waited. Although we were not the highest bid—and there had been a lot of interest, they picked us as we were very local to the plot. It all went through, with the usual level of solicitor back and forth. Not overly stressful on its own, but it was something else that needed our overextended attention.

We had not deliberately taken on all these projects at the same time, but some had stretched out far longer than planned—and you can never really predict other issues. We had definitely allowed ourselves to take on far more than we could cope with at once.

And then came the health scares…

I found a lump and went to the doctor. **Concerned about the possibility of cancer**, he booked me in for blood tests and ultrasound at a nearby hospital. My situation created an immediate cloud of uncertainty…waiting for that month seemed like an eternity.

Fortunately, the results of the scan turned out less dire than we feared, but it was still a rollercoaster of emotions. The doctor cautioned me to keep monitoring it, and to come back if it changed.

The next month, Sarah went to the doctor for hormonal issues she was experiencing. After a scan, **the doctor found an enormous mass, and told her "it might be cancer!"** It felt like we had been kicked, when we were already down on the floor.

For the next few months, Sarah underwent a barrage of tests and scans. Her abdomen had swollen so much that it looked like she was pregnant—but she definitely wasn't.

Eventually, Sarah had an MRI. Fortunately, after reviewing the scans, they decided it wasn't cancer, but a 5-inch wide ovarian cyst. Due to its size, she would need major surgery, but we didn't have any idea when that would take place.

Every day seemed to bring a fresh wave of stress. **I found myself struggling more and more to cope with life.**

As if that wasn't enough to deal with, our son's entry into secondary (middle) school was a huge transition—especially given his special needs. Although he appeared to settle in his first few weeks, the calm quickly turned into a storm. He was in a state of constant stress. The school couldn't give him the personal attention and support he needed. He resisted going to school, and **every day, we faced explosive outbursts at home, during which he would swear, hit, and destroy things.** Every morning and evening felt like a tornado wreaking havoc in our lives.

As the next two months unfolded, the situation reached a breaking point. Sarah and I rarely argue, but she wanted to home educate him—and I was concerned we would be failing him by pulling him out of the school system. **We argued about it for months, creating even more tension in an already stressed-out home life**. The toll on my son's mental health, and consequently ours, was becoming unbearable.

Eventually I reluctantly agreed that pulling him out of school was not just an option, but necessary to protect him from the emotional trauma he was enduring. We decided to home-educate his sister too, as she was only intermittently coping with school.

Dealing with a highly traumatized special needs child, navigating the intricacies of home-educating, and the constant worry about Sarah's upcoming surgery—it seemed like we were teetering on the edge of a crisis!

Sarah broke down, "We can't go on like this! Something has to give!"

We'd pushed ourselves to take on more and more projects every year, with endless to-do lists, in the pursuit of success. When we'd run out of things to do, we created more projects to start.

Amidst the chaos, we realized it was time to reassess our priorities. Our illnesses were a sign from the Universe, Mother Nature, Divinity, God, or whatever label you prefer. We'd accepted and received the message loud and clear, like a slap in the face…we needed to slow down. The next question was "How?"

Sarah's meditations echoed a simple solution: "Simplify, simplify, simplify..." And so, we dubbed the next phase of our lives, "The year of Simplicity." We'd built a really complicated life. How on earth could we unpick it? Little did we know at the time, that we would create the Simplicity Secret Tool, a topic we'll delve into in the upcoming chapters.

Embracing simplicity meant dismantling the intricacies of our overly complicated life. Considering we owned multiple properties and small companies, this seemed daunting. But we embraced the Simplicity Secret, vowing to make decisions aligned with our newfound vision. We estimated a three-year timeline for us. Others might simplify their lives in just a few months—but for us, there was a long journey ahead.

We did an emergency stop and slammed the brakes on everything! Our first major decision was to stop all remortgaging.

We gave up! The mortgage companies didn't want to lend right now, and it was too frustrating for us. We'd remortgage them another time. That lifted a huge weight off our mind and stopped the endless back and forth with the finance companies.

Our next decision was to close our property training company the following year, when our tax year ended. That would open up a huge amount of free time. Closing the company was a really sad decision, as we we'd helped many people to reach financial freedom. In the meantime, we informed all our students that we were closing, and stopped accepting new mentees. Month by month, we began winding down mentoring calls. We cut down posting on social media and stopped producing our weekly videos.

We didn't do anything with the agricultural property we'd bought as our potential new home. We owned it, but we let it sit there.

This gave us much more bandwidth to cope with everything else.

Recognising that our emotional state wasn't objective, we put together a 3-year plan to simplify our life—then met with our mentor to discuss it. Because of taxes, leases, and market cycles, we were looking at a long time period to complete our plan.

This plan became our anchor, providing a clear path through the storm. Just having the plan created a sense of relief. We put together a meticulous spreadsheet outlining each step, ticking off tasks day-by-day. We removed layer upon layer of complexities in our life.

We decided to sell two properties the next year, in order to close another company. We planned to use the proceeds to fund building our new sustainable home in the countryside, rather than having to get a self-build mortgage.

We spoke to our Architect and began designing plans to build our new home. Although it added some complexity, it would result in us owning one less property, and give us a sustainable and low maintenance base for our family.

We closed our training company just in time for Sarah's surgery. **The operation was successful, but more extensive than planned**, due to complications. I felt waves of emotions as I sat by her bedside, witnessing her drift in and out of consciousness—and vomit all over her gown and the bed. When visiting hours ended, I made the sombre drove home, where Sarah's parents were looking after our worried children.

I visited Sarah every day until she could return home. **She couldn't do much more than sit or lie down for many months**. Even seven months later, she still occasionally experiences pain on long drives.

It was at this crossroads that we vowed to create a simpler life. One where we could manage the emotional storms—and as a number one priority, maintain the physical and mental health of our family.

Instead of rapidly expanding, we would restrict the number of projects we took on. **We also completed yoga instructor and meditation teaching qualifications, to build a toolkit for balancing our stress levels.**

Our two kids were significantly happier being home-educated, resulting in a much calmer home life. It took long time for their emotional scars to heal, but they're in a much better place now.

In terms of new projects, **we've been careful about selecting which projects to start, and making sure we don't take on too many simultaneously.** Since we started simplifying, we've been feeling far less stressed, and more in control of our lives.

We're about halfway through our initial three-year plan, and each step is freeing up more and more time, as we continue to simplify. It's given us the bandwidth and passion to write this book, as we felt that we needed to get the message out to other people with stressful lives.

As we navigated these changes, the complexity of our former life gradually unravelled, revealing the path ahead to serenity and fulfilment.

CHAPTER 2

Free Bonus Content

To provide you with the most value, we've also included a wealth of high-value bonus material for free, including:

✓ Domino Action Plan template
✓ Manifesting Your Dream Life Meditation
✓ Yoga Nidra Meditation (Yogic Nap)
✓ Simplicity tools we use—save time and money
✓ Follow guests in Simplicity Secret
✓ Books mentioned in Simplicity Secret
✓ If I Die template
✓ Bumble Bee breath tutorial for stress relief

REGISTER FOR FREE ACCESS NOW:
bit.ly/ss-bonus-content

Developing Your Vision

CHAPTER 3

"Create the highest, grandest vision possible for your life because you become what you believe."
—Oprah Winfrey

How Are You Feeling Right Now?

If you're completely freaking out today, then perhaps jump to *Tools to Reduce Overwhelm and Stress* in Chapter 10—then return here to develop your vision.

Creating Three Months of Joy

Alright, let's ignite the fire within and create a roadmap to a brighter future!

Life can feel like off-roading, and we all find ourselves in the ditch from time to time. Both Sarah and I have experienced times when we were really overwhelmed and felt that we had nothing to look forward to. Sometimes it was really difficult to get out of this funk.

But remember, the view from the peak is breath-taking, and you deserve to experience it.

We've used the following exercise many times, to lift our spirits and give us hope in tough times.

Now, let's transform a blank sheet of paper into a beacon of positivity. In the centre, write **"3 Months of Joy."** This is your compass, guiding you through the next three months with excitement and joy.

Imagine this as your personal mind map, a constellation of joy waiting to be explored. Start by adding spokes and bubbles radiating from the centre—each bubble representing a pleasurable experience that awaits you. **Let the first wave of bubbles come from activities you can dive into today**—simple pleasures that light up your world.

Perhaps it's immersing yourself in your favourite uplifting TV show, savouring a delicious meal at a local restaurant, or indulging in the serenity of a spa day. Picture yourself strolling along the beach, feeling the sand beneath your feet, or planning a rejuvenating weekend getaway. These are the building blocks of your roadmap to joy. **Make sure that it's achievable, and affordable.** Many things can be free or cheap to do.

Now, extend your mind map into the coming weeks, and up to three months ahead. What future adventures make your heart race with excitement? Whether it's attending a concert, starting a new hobby, or reconnecting with old friends, let your imagination run wild. The key is to fill your map with activities that fuel your positivity.

Crucially, ensure that many of these items can be checked off in the short term. Immediate gratification is the secret sauce to lift your spirits swiftly. This isn't just a plan—it's a commitment to your own well-being.

Once your mind map is complete, don't let it gather dust. **Place it where your eyes meet it daily**, a constant reminder of the joy awaiting you.

And here's the crucial part—take deliberate steps to turn these dreams into reality.

Embrace the power of this mind map and let the next three months be overflowing with joy and purpose. You've got this!

ENVISIONING A SIMPLIFIED AND FULFILLING LIFE

Now that you've identified some things that light you up, it's time to craft a vision for a simplified and fulfilling life. Picture your life full of ease and flow. **Simplification doesn't mean sacrificing your dreams—rather, it's about prioritizing what truly matters.**

While keeping in mind your values and passions, consider the areas of your life—finances, career, relationships, home life, health and fitness. What would it look like with a more balanced and fulfilling existence? Simplicity is the key to reducing overwhelm—making room for the things that bring you joy.

Visualize your ideal day. Remember, simplicity is about focusing on the essential, while eliminating the rest. It's a deliberate choice to lead a life that aligns with your values and passions.

Be aspirational in your vision—but don't ten times your current lifestyle, such as winning the lottery, as your brain just screams bullshit! So, if you're broke and you try to imagine yourself flying around in a private jet, you'll find it difficult to believe it can happen.

Grab a pen and paper and write down your vision. Be as specific as possible about how you'd spend your days.

Perhaps you're travelling around the world, spending all morning on wellness, walking your kids to school, starting a new hobby, volunteering at an animal sanctuary, or having a zero-loan balance. **It doesn't need to be perfect**. You'll likely adjust it as you journey through this book. **All you need to do is make a start.**

A simplified life is not about perfection, but progress. So, embrace the journey and savour the moments of growth and transformation.

THE SCIENCE OF MANIFESTING YOUR DREAM LIFE

Now that you've visualised your dream life, mental rehearsal is the rocket fuel for launching your dreams into reality! Many Olympic athletes swear by this tool.

Picture this: perhaps you want that dream job? Close your eyes, feel the weight of the office key in your hand, hear the hum of productivity around you. Mental rehearsal allows you to step into the shoes of your future self, to see and experience success before it materialises. This isn't mere wishful thinking; it's a powerful technique that aligns your thoughts, beliefs, and actions with your aspirations.

These aren't daydreams. This is strategic, focused rehearsal in the theatre of your mind. When you vividly see yourself conquering those goals, you're not wishing—you're programming your mind for success!

So, let's make it happen! **Dive into the 20-minute Manifesting Your Dream Life Meditation from the Bonus Content in Chapter 2** and watch as your dream life unfolds before your eyes. bit.ly/ss-bonus-content

Listen to it every day for 21 days and witness the transformation. It's not magic; it's science! By vividly imagining your goals and desired outcomes, you're not just fantasizing; you're laying the groundwork for reality.

When you try to meditate, **if your brain is going around and around on a negative issue**, then you may find it difficult to visualise right now.

If that's happening today, then use the **Yoga Nidra meditation in the Bonus Content area, to give your mind and body the break it needs right now.**

Creating Your Simplicity Plan

DOMINO ACTION PLAN

Identifying the one big Domino is like finding that pivotal element with the power to transform your life. It's like the "One Ring to Rule Them All," from The Lord of the Rings. It's a single force with the potential to eradicate dissatisfaction, and steer you towards happiness.

Ask yourself: is most of your dissatisfaction at work?

Maybe your boss is a source of misery?

Does your job lack fulfilment?

Is your daily commute tedious?

The One Domino in this scenario might be getting a different job closer to home, more aligned with your passions. By knocking over this one Domino, you create a cascading effect, knocking down multiple discontentment dominos.

For example, our One Domino was to close our property training company. In one fell swoop, we removed the stress of constant launches, weekly mentoring meetings, answering daily messages, admin, accounting, and much more—this gave Sarah and I the bandwidth to move our focus to our health issues.

As we step through the five areas of life in Simplicity Secret, keep domino goals in mind. Perhaps you'll identify not just one, but two or three dominos that, when toppled, have the potential to solve a significant number of dissatisfiers in different parts of your life.

It's about taking strategic action, not wishful thinking—so skip things like winning the lottery. Instead, focus on tangible steps you can take to set off a chain reaction of positive changes.

Lengthy action plans look great, but in our experience a simple one-page summary works best. Make sure you refer to every day, or at least once a week, to make huge progress. It keeps you focused on the most important goals. It is one of the key secrets behind us achieving so much in our life.

Just by making a plan, you can move from feeling like a victim of your circumstances, to taking back your power and control of the situation. When we put together our 3-year plan, we immediately felt a huge sense of relief, even though we hadn't actioned any of it yet. We'd moved from fear, to empowerment. It gave us the momentum to start doing challenging tasks!

Introducing our Domino Action Plan, or as we refer to it at home— "The Plan." **We've included a blank template for you to fill out in the Bonus Content area of Chapter 2** bit.ly/ss-bonus-content

Fill out this template as you read through this book, so you can make sure you capture the goals you plan to implement.

There are four key areas in the Domino Action Plan (DAP): Vision, 1 year, 3 years and Rules.

a) Vision

Take the vision you created, and write a simplified bullet-point version into the DAP. This vision is the destination you want to get to. Make sure you also include WHY you want to achieve this.

b) 1 Year

What are the key goals to simplify your life over the next 12 months? And what elements can you add back in for more fulfilment?

Consider all areas: Money, Work and Mission, Relationships, Home Life, and Health and Fitness. Focus on quick wins, or where there is the most pain. Ensure your goals are a steppingstone to achieve your vision.

Choose big domino goals that fix a lot of issues in one go. Whether that's selling your barely used second car to pay off debts, joining a specific community aligned with your biggest passion, paying a mentor to help you grow your business, buying your first rental property, or putting £200 a month into savings for your "Courage Pot."

When you find yourself distracted, endlessly scrolling on social media, or tinkering with a website, check the DAP to see whether there is something you could do to really move the needle in your life today.

c) 3 Years

Not every goal can be achieved in the first year. Sometimes you need to wait for a change in the market, or other things to happen on a set date before you can complete the goal. Examples could be:

downsizing your home when your child turns 18 years old; selling off your property portfolio to retire; or tidying up your affairs to go travelling around the world. Even if it takes you three years to complete a significant goal, there will be some elements you can achieve within the first year—so include those specific elements there. Check your goals align with your vision.

If circumstances change—don't be afraid to pivot and revise your goals in the DAP. You may find that something doesn't resonate any more, or you discover something more inspiring to do. We review our goals monthly, but also make tweaks as we go along. Just don't change your mind every week, as you won't get anywhere!

d) Rules

Over the years, Sarah and I have noticed certain patterns in our life when things went really bad! **This led us to create rules to follow, so that we don't make the same mistakes again.**

For instance, we have a rule for the size of our savings Courage Pot. Whenever we've dipped below this level in the past, we've often regretted it, as we were constantly worried whether we could pay the bills.

> *"Change your story, change your life."*
> *—Tony Robbins*

We all have stories we tell ourselves. And when we keep telling ourselves the same stories, it blinds us to what is truly possible for us.

We tell ourselves something won't work for us because we're: poor, broke, stupid, ugly, attractive, don't have time, have kids, don't have kids, single, married, young, old, thin, fat, tall, short, my life is harder than anyone else's, I can't move, I can't change jobs, everyone is against me, I'm worthless, and so on.

These create beliefs that are not true. Whenever you say to yourself 'always' or 'never,' and 'I've tried everything,' also ask yourself, 'Is it really true? Would other people agree with you? Is it actually a story you tell yourself—leading to the same patterns in your life, over and over again? But there is hope…

Think of a time in your life where you broke a negative pattern. You've done this before and can do it again. Recognising a pattern removes your fear. You can make a breakthrough by setting rules for a new pattern. So, I invite you to reflect on your life, and look for those mistakes you've made over and over again. **Design your rules for living, to create a simpler, stress-free, and fulfilling life. You can do this! We've got you.**

When you're feeling stressed out and overwhelmed, sometimes just taking on one goal feels too much—so be kind to yourself. Tackle something easy. Every day we aim to take one small step towards each of our goals—if that's possible. It could be as little as booking a meeting with someone, or researching a topic.

LIMIT YOUR PROJECTS

One of the rules in our Domino Action Plan is a maximum of three big projects shared between the two of us.

While we have more than three domino goals in our one-year plan, we aim to only have three of them active at the same time. This creates a bit of space for those unknown issues that always seem to crop up.

If a project is really complicated, then it can be beneficial to use project management software, or simply list the tasks in a spreadsheet and tick them off as you achieve them—which feels great! There were a huge number of steps to close one of our businesses, so we used a spreadsheet for that.

Once you've completed a project, you have more bandwidth to start another.

CHAPTER 4

Unlocking the Simplicity Secret

DISSATISFIERS

Our brains are wired in a way that makes us pay more attention to the negative aspects of life—it's what we call the "negativity bias."

Think of it as an ancient survival mechanism. If our ancestors heard a lion's roar, they didn't stop to smell the roses…they ran for their lives!

Now, fast forward to the present, and the media knows this bias well. Ever notice how headlines are mostly dominated by negative news? Not only that, but the negative headline is often a huge exaggeration of the facts. Check it out next time you dive into the news.

Now, let me ask you a question: Have you ever had a day that started off fantastic, only to be derailed by one or two little things?

Suddenly, those minor hiccups take centre stage, overshadowing all the good stuff. It feels like your whole day is ruined, and everything else fades into the background.

Here's the game-changer—imagine ditching those joy-sucking elements from your life. I'm talking about eliminating those dissatisfiers that you've been putting up with.

We define a dissatisfier as something that constantly annoys you, not one-off events you can't control. For instance, an unreliable car that breaks down all the time. Or a long, irritating commute to work.

And guess what? Fixing one of these is way more effective at boosting your happiness, than the temporary high of buying or experiencing something new.

So, let's roll up our sleeves and dive into what's been dragging you down.

Grab a sheet of paper and draw 5 columns with the following headings:

1. Finances and Assets

2. Career and Mission

3. Relationships

4. Home life

5. Health & Fitness

Write down all the joy-crushing dissatisfiers in your life and circle the ones that are the worst! We're not just listing them for fun—we're gearing up to kick them to the curb.

Your happiness is on the line, and we're about to turn the tables on those dissatisfiers.

Get ready for a life upgrade!

Simplicity Secret Tool

"When you're stressed, simplify the rest."
—George Choy

Every time you come up against a dissatisfier in your everyday life, use the *Simplicity Secret Tool*:

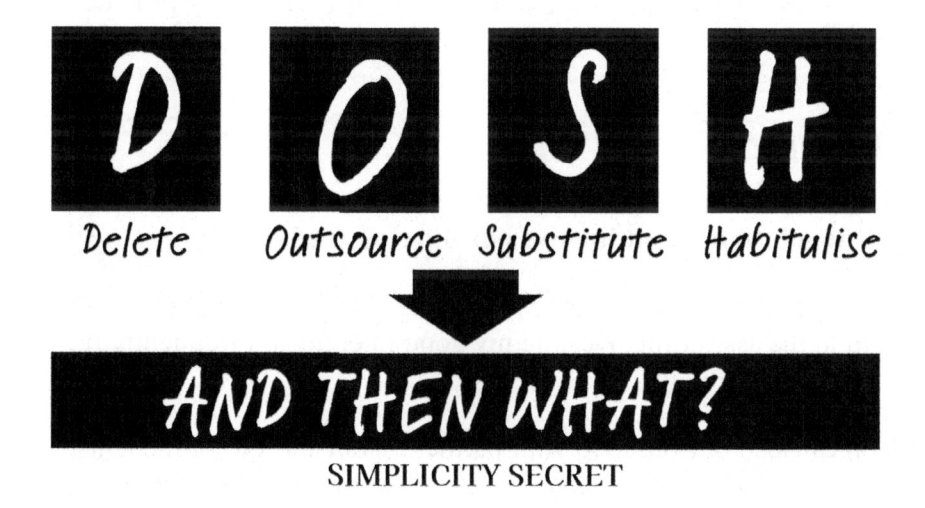

D Delete **O** Outsource **S** Substitute **H** Habitulise

⬇

AND THEN WHAT?

SIMPLICITY SECRET

Delete

What if I told you that the key to maximizing your happiness lies in the art of deletion?

What if you could only delete?

Perhaps your website homepage is bustling with myriad clickable options, and seemingly endless scrolling. After conducting a meticulous analysis of user interactions, you reveal a surprising revelation—most of the clicks are from just two buttons. Imagine the increase in clickthrough rate after eliminating the unnecessary, and condensing your content to just one screen.

Next, let's give an example in your home. Picture the delicate china crockery in the display cabinet—remnants of a joyous wedding gift, meticulously preserved for that "special occasion." Welcome to my life! Anyway, when was the last time we used that china? Our crockery had been sitting untouched, collecting dust for years. We had to pack them up every time we moved. Finally, we decided to sell them—released them into the world where they could be cherished and used regularly by someone else.

If you can only choose one part of DOSH, Delete usually provides the best results.

Outsource

Sometimes, when faced with a dissatisfier, and you can't delete it, the solution might involve outsourcing the issue.

I love my car, but the lengthy process of washing the outside is a real pain in the ass for me. Despite my good intentions, I frequently find myself driving to the car wash.

You can also outsource to your partner. Sarah and I have recognised and embraced our different skill sets, creating a complementary and more effective team. Years ago, we took the initiative to list tasks we enjoyed or disliked, both at home and work—then strategically assigned responsibilities.

For instance, I've taken on the role of handling all things technology-related within our family. I'm the designated "Tech support" for any computer issues Sarah or our kids encounter. Sarah is in charge of our kids' home education.

Sarah used to manage rental properties, when she worked at an Estate and Lettings Agent. However, we made a conscious decision years ago to outsource the management of our properties, giving us the freedom to reclaim our time.

Sometimes, our pride keeps us from accepting assistance. Your mother might have offered to watch your children countless times, yet you've hesitated to take her up on it. Meanwhile, you're worn out and in need of a break. **Could now be the moment to set aside your pride** and take her up on her kind offer to help?

SUBSTITUTE

Substituting what you have for something better, can sometimes fix a major dissatisfier.

Consider this: if your valuable time, mental energy, and hard-earned cash are taken up by the ceaseless upkeep of your elderly car—then maybe it's time to substitute it for a more reliable option.

Similarly, if the constant ads on your TV are driving you crazy, maybe it's time to check out other TV subscriptions that let you watch without annoying interruptions.

HABITUALISE (AUTOMATE)

In certain situations, taking charge of a task you're not thrilled about may be the only way to resolve a dissatisfier.

To create a habit, I use a technique I call "event stacking." Basically, you attach a new habit you want to form, to a routine event in your day or week.

For example, let's say you want to make meditation a regular practice, but struggle to stick with it. Try waking up, going to the bathroom, and then meditating for 20 minutes in bed. It gets done before the hustle and bustle of your day kicks in, eliminating the excuses.

If motivation is a challenge, create a list of 50 ways it will benefit you. Push yourself to list all 50, to really feel the impact.

You can also set up automation tools, so tasks happen without you thinking about them. A simple example is an automated bank transfer each month, to your savings account.

And Then What?

Having explored DOSH, let's now delve into the transformative question: And Then What?

"And then What" is your gateway to the realms of your Future and Fulfilment

i) **Future**

Imagine this scenario: You've pinpointed a dissatisfier in your life, applied the principles of DOSH, and reached a decision. Now, project yourself into the future and ask the compelling question, "And then what?" **Envision the reality of living with your choice. Delve into the potential downsides.** Scrutinize whether your decision truly resolved the issue, or birthed a new set of challenges.

Here's a personal example: I used to travel once or twice a month by train to work, leaving my car parked at the station for a few days. Sarah wasn't travelling with me, so we bought an additional small manual transmission car for the task.

It seemed practical until we realised two things. Firstly, the costs—depreciation, insurance and parking surpassed my earnings from the business trips. Secondly, the cheap manual gearbox, chosen for frugality, made driving really unsatisfying.

If only we'd considered "And Then What?" Eventually, we chose to eliminate the problem. We sold the second car and, for occasional trips to the train station, I hired Sarah's mother to drive me. By deleting the car, we saved a substantial amount of money and hassle!

ii) **Fulfilment**

Once you've streamlined your life, don't stop there; ask yourself again, "And then what?"

With your newfound freedom, resist the temptation to complicate matters—as we'll admit, we did upon achieving financial freedom. Instead, channel your inner curiosity and ask, "And Then What?"

Add in elements aligned with your passions and values. Transform your freedom into a more fulfilling and purpose-driven life.

We'll give you some suggestions for a more fulfilling life towards the end of this book.

Decision Fatigue Results In Crap Decisions

"The quality of your decisions determines the quality of your life"
—Tony Robbins

From the moment your alarm wakes you, the decision-making marathon commences. Running low on toilet paper triggers the first call to action—need to buy more. What would I like for breakfast? Should I wear the white or blue shirt? What should I eat for lunch? Even mundane traffic forces us to consider alternate routes. Social media pings, text messages, and emails continually draw from your decision reserves. **While some estimates suggest we make up to 35,000 decisions per day**, the sheer volume is staggering.

DECISION FATIGUE

Graph: Decision Quality (y-axis) vs Decisions Quantity (x-axis), showing a sharply declining curve. At top left: "I'm the boss!" At bottom right: "Oh crap!! What did I do?"

SIMPLICITY SECRET

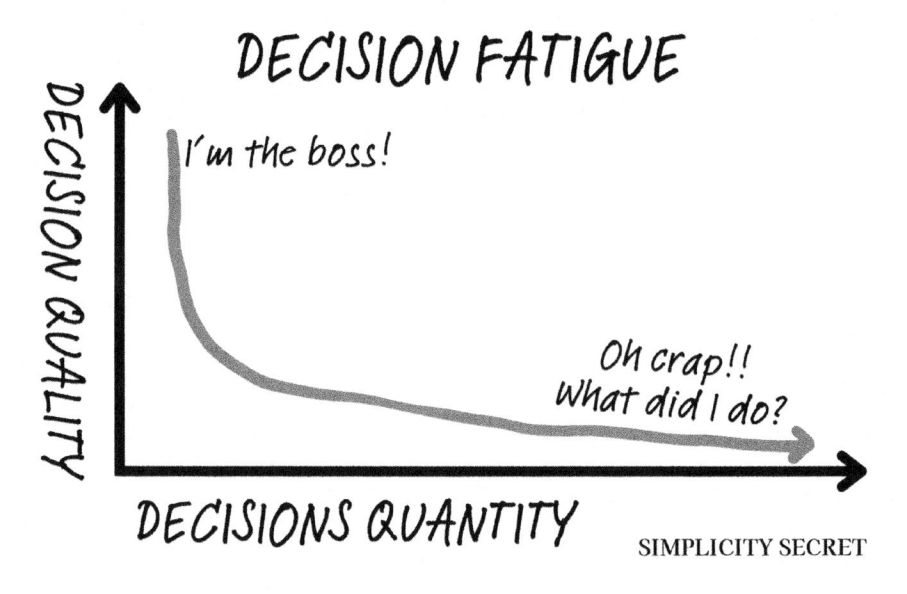

Imagine your mind as a "decision" bank with a fluctuating balance. Every choice, whether trivial or substantial, chips away at this reserve. Not only that, **but as the quantity of decisions increases throughout the day, our decision-making ability gets worse, resulting in crap decisions.** Decision fatigue is one reason we feel overwhelmed.[2] Well-rested days replenish the balance, but overwhelming workloads or complex tasks, rapidly deplete it.

Sleepless nights worsen the situation, resulting in a reduced balance upon waking. The mental fatigue from constant decision-making can lead to irritability, or the feeling of having nothing more to give. The toll on our mental reserves underscores **the importance of reducing the number of daily decisions** we make on tiresome tasks.

People say they want choice—but often we become overwhelmed by the number of choices. Take for example when I was looking for some tortilla chips in the local supermarket. All I wanted to do was quickly grab some humous and chips for lunch. I stood there for 10 minutes as I looked at the back of each of the 48 packets of different chips. No, this one has milk…no this one has too many artificial ingredients…do I want chili? By the end of it I felt exhausted by the choices. "Just give me some tortilla chips!"

Many top performers have embraced simplicity to combat decision fatigue. Co-founder of Apple, Steve Jobs, famously wore a black turtleneck and jeans every day.

Mark Zuckerberg, co-founder of Facebook and Meta adopts a similar approach, sporting jeans with a grey T-shirt. By minimizing mundane decisions, these leaders conserve mental energy for higher priority work.

I was a Personal Trainer for a couple of years—and I remember the great relief from wearing my company branded gym clothes every day. I didn't have to think in the mornings, and as an added bonus, people would approach me in the street for training. Even now, Sarah and I maintain a very limited wardrobe, which makes it quick to get dressed in the morning.

So, in your day-to-day life, set the intention to always be looking for ways to eliminate decisions you regularly make.

Now, brace yourselves for the upcoming chapters on **the five pillars of life: Money, Work and Mission, Relationships, Home Life, and Health and Fitness.**

Armed with the wisdom and tools you've gleaned from the first four chapters, I want you to dive deep into the abyss of your painful reality.

Identify the areas that are causing you the most turmoil. Write them on your Domino Action Plan as you progress through this book.

Now, here's the game-changer—**take immediate action, no matter how modest, to secure a quick win.** It could be a small step, a bold decision, or a big domino move. The key is to break the chains and start the momentum toward a life of abundance and fulfilment.

Get ready to ignite the fire within and blaze a trail towards your dream life! Remember…

Don't overthink it—use Simplicity Secret.

CHAPTER 5

Make More Money

Warning: Investing in financial markets and alternative investments involves inherent risks, and past performance is not indicative of future results. Your capital is at risk. Please seek the advice of a qualified financial professional and tax advisor before making investment decisions. Seek advice of a debt professional if you are having problems paying your debts.

> *"The first rule of an investment is don't lose [money]. And the second rule of an investment is don't forget the first rule."*
> *— Warren Buffet*

In this chapter on money, we're diving deep into the realms of mastering your finances—from the art of saving, paying off debts, managing your expenses, the science of strategic investing, all the way through to planning for retirement.

We're going to simplify money to show you what the wealthy do. Get ready for a comprehensive journey toward financial empowerment and abundance! There's also a lovely interview with yoga teacher, Diana Finch-Keran on how she simplified her finances after leaving the corporate world. Oh, and we'll share many of our failures to keep you entertained!

If you would like to learn more about how to manage your money, please read one of our other books:
Stealth Millionaire: How to Save and Manage Your Money Like the Rich

No matter where you are in your financial freedom journey, I invite you to be open to one thing: **"I am in control of my cost of living."**

No matter what you think you "need to buy," these are the choices you make every day. If you move back in with your parents, then your costs go down. If you move to a cheaper country, then your expenses reduce. You don't *have* to send your kids to private school; you don't *have* to book a vacation; you don't *have* to spend a fortune on birthdays and Christmas. **Everything is a decision.** What you're really looking for is happiness, and that, can be found inside you. The Buddhists have known this for over 2,500 years. In the words of the Buddha:

> *"The secret of happiness lies in mind's release from worldly ties."*
> —The Buddha

This means that the constant craving for things, creates suffering. If you can recognise and break the cycle, you can achieve a happier life. Many of the things that bring you the most joy and fulfilment, don't cost much at all. As you start your journey through the topic of money, keep the Simplicity Secret Tool in mind:

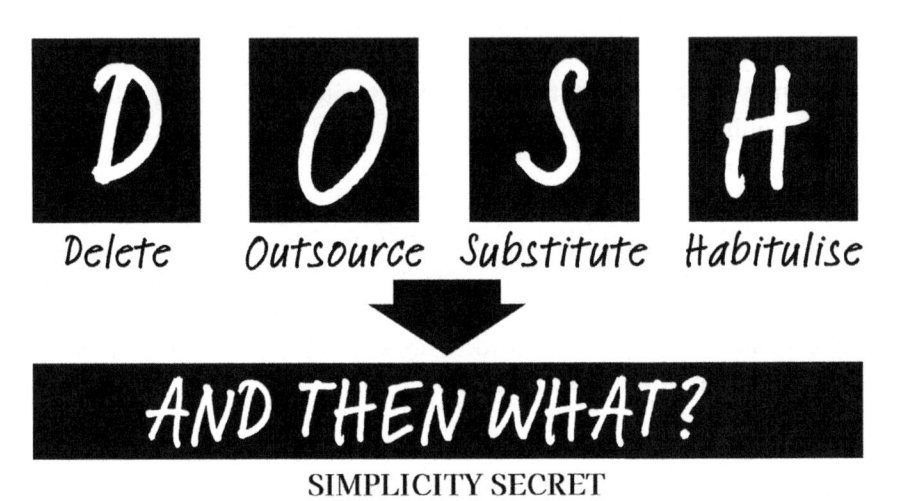

D Delete **O** Outsource **S** Substitute **H** Habitulise

⬇

AND THEN WHAT?

SIMPLICITY SECRET

Mastering the Art of Saving: Your Path to Financial Freedom

Your Courage Pot (Savings)

When your savings are running on empty, it's like having a grumpy guest who never leaves—stress and worry keep knocking on your door every day!

Over the years, we've experienced numerous highs and lows. There were times when we were barely scraping by, struggling to afford food. Every minute of the day was filled with the constant hum of financial stress. This created a lot of complexity—juggling money and constantly thinking about whether we could pay the bills.

We've learned from this mistake, and now affectionately refer to our savings as the "Courage Pot," because it gives us courage in times of need. It provides comforting security, preventing impulsive decisions due to feeling desperate.

Let's be realistic—unexpected expenses are inevitable. Given that only half of Brits have up to £1,000 in savings, and a quarter have none at all, it's understandable why people resort to expensive loans or only paying minimum credit card payments each month.[3]

Economic uncertainties occur in cycles, from property and stock market crashes, to high unemployment and substantial interest rate hikes. We've personally weathered the storm of having half of our rental properties vacant simultaneously!

Then there are those truly unpredictable events like the pandemic—black swans and unexpected twists in life that can seriously mess with your finances. That's where liquid cash becomes your financial superhero.

To prepare for such uncertainties, having liquid cash is essential. Ask yourself: how long you could survive without income?

Or what if your business folded?

What if you needed a new car?

Our suggestion is to build your Courage Pot to at least three months' worth of your personal, or small business expenses—whichever is the greater.

And if you want more reassurance for your family, aim for a whole year's worth tucked away in a high-interest savings account or other cash equivalent.

Sure, there are people out there who say, "Invest everything and forget about cash!" But from our personal experiences, dipping into our Courage Pot without a backup plan has left us stressed and wondering if we can pay the bills on time.

Surely the rich wouldn't hold that much in cash? What about the returns? It may surprise you to know that there are **people with an average net worth of $100 million who hold an average of three years of their annual living expenses in cash**, or cash equivalent.[4] However, I imagine that they probably have only one year as their Courage Pot, and the other two years is a "War Chest" of cash to jump on any investment opportunities. That is next level!

Your Courage Pot should be easily accessible—whether in a high-interest savings account, gold, silver, watches, or any asset quickly convertible to cash. If you have a non-cash asset, make sure you really know the market and can liquidate it fast. I advise caution against keeping it in stocks, as markets crash rapidly during black swan events. Fixed income investments, like bonds, offer slightly more stability, though their values still fluctuate.

Having a Courage Pot ensures that, in the worst-case scenario of zero income, you can survive with a roof over your head and food on the table. It serves as a stress buffer, keeping you grounded when life throws unexpected challenges your way. Your Courage Pot is your sanity saver!

HABITUALISE YOUR SAVINGS

You might be thinking, "Sure, telling me to save three months' worth of expenses in cash is easy for you to say, but how do I actually do it?"

Well, fear not, because **there are two great ways** to make this happen.

OPTION 1: FORCED SAVING

Kick off your Courage Pot savings by **setting up an automatic monthly transfer from your current account (or chequing account), to your savings account.**

Start with an amount that fits comfortably within your budget. Even £10 a month is an investment in your future. Soon enough, you'll adapt to this routine, and you won't even notice the money leaving your account.

Dr John Demartini, the Human Behaviour Expert, suggests a savvy strategy—**increase the transferred amount by 10% every three months.** This gradual increase accelerates your savings in quick time.

To instil good investment habits in our children, we've adopted a forced saving approach. We impose a 50% tax on their pocket money and any money gifts, by putting it into their stock market "house fund." That way they are investing in their future.

OPTION 2: NOTICE BOARD SAVINGS

Make your savings goal impossible to ignore, by putting your current and target savings figures on your notice board, fridge, or anywhere you glance at frequently.

Create a simple spreadsheet or grab a notebook to record your total savings each month. We've recorded our savings for many years. This visual record not only motivates you, but also shows you how close you are to your target savings amount.

Habitualise Your Credit Cards

When I got my first job, I had no clue about managing my money, so I racked up credit card debt and car finance loans. It felt like my entire paycheque vanished each month, and I could barely keep up with the minimum payments on my credit card.

Later, I worked in the credit card industry, where I discovered that the interest rates for sticking to the **minimum monthly payment are some of the most punishing you'll ever encounter**. Paying only the minimum amount each month puts you in a cycle that could keep you in debt FOREVER.

Here's my suggestion: opt for a debit card, restricting your spending to what's in your bank account. **Alternatively, set up your credit card for automatic full monthly payments**—it's what I do and most card companies provide this option. That way there is no choice. You have to pay off the full balance every month. It also lifts the burden off your decision fatigue, as you have no choice but to pay it in full.

Conquering Debts: The Road to Liberation

Pay Off Your Debts

Now it goes without saying, if you are struggling with your debts, then seek advice from a debt professional.

Alright, envision two categories of debts in your financial journey. **First up, the "Good Debts"—these fund profitable investments.** Think of buying a rental property with a mortgage—ensuring that the overall return after expenses aligns with your financial goals.

Now, let's talk about the "Bad Debts," the high-interest culprits like credit cards, car loans, and fancy sofa finance. **These are loans on depreciating assets**, or just your household spend. These are the silent wealth killers. Aim to swiftly clear out all those bad debts and pave the way to a simpler financial life.

There are many different ways you can clear your debts. **One approach is to "Substitute," by consolidating all your debts into a single loan at a lower rate.** Some people also choose remortgage their home to pay off debts, but obviously your house is at risk when you do this. Both of those options have the advantage of simplifying the number of debt providers you are working with and reduce decision fatigue.

You can also consider transferring a balance from one credit card to another, **by choosing one with a 0% interest rate on balance transfers.** Although this can save you money, it doesn't simplify your finances. When your time limit runs out you will be back to the shocking interest rate again. **And don't assume you will be accepted for another card.**

Consider the cautionary tale of a friend of mine who accumulated £90,000 in credit card debt at 0% interest, only to be denied further balance transfers. Stuck with a sky-high interest rate for many years, he found it extremely difficult to clear it.

Should you pay off the highest interest rate first?

When deciding which debts to prioritize, two schools of thought emerge. Of course, paying off the most expensive rate first will maximise your cashflow. But sometimes eliminating the smallest loan amount first, can provide a quick win and boost morale by simplifying the number of loans you have and reducing decision fatigue. See which option feels right for you.

Streamline Your Accounts

I once knew someone with a staggering 100 financial accounts! Every time he came across a high-interest rate account, or a promising fund performance, he'd eagerly open a new account and put some money in it. He never closed anything! However, as the years went by, managing this extensive portfolio became increasingly complex. Can you imagine how much mail he received every day? He found himself overwhelmed with paperwork and filing, leading to letters and money being misplaced.

His financial complexity needed to be simplified. After enduring three years of waiting for fixed terms to end, the number of accounts was reduced from over 100 to a more manageable 4 accounts.

Ask yourself: can you simplify your financial accounts, by consolidating them?

Conquering Expenses for a Richer Tomorrow

The Art of Simplifying Expenses and Decluttering Your Life

In a world inundated with advertisements promising a happier existence through material possessions, it's no wonder that we buy things we don't need—and fill our house with stuff.

> *"People buy feelings, not things"*
> —Tony Robbins

Tony Robbins says the *6 Human Needs* "drive every decision you make"—whether fulfilled in a positive or negative way. Many of our deepest needs are developed during our childhood, creating our beliefs and values. **The 6 Human Needs are:**

1. Certainty: knowing what will happen. For example, getting a regular paycheque, or habits that give you the same feeling when you do them.

2. Uncertainty/Variety: need for the unknown. Trying new or risky things.

3. Significance: wanting to feel unique, important, special, or higher status.

4. Love and Connection: feel closeness to someone, a pet, or something higher than you.

5. Growth: expanding your knowledge or capabilities.

6. Contribution: helping and supporting others, or service.

Buying luxury items to show off to other people, in an attempt to raise your status means that you have a high need for significance.

This is often to fill a void of having low self-esteem inside. I've been there! I felt "poor" for most of my life.

Buying stuff does not make you happy for very long, if at all. Tony Robbins advises that real fulfilment comes from addressing the last three human needs: Love and connection, growth and contribution.

If you have enough self-awareness of your current thought patterns and a desire to change, then you can refocus your human needs to achieve a more fulfilling life.

Consider the shirt you recently purchased—perhaps it was an attempt to feel more attractive (*Love*), or the new Mercedes—a pursuit of *significance*. Discretionary spend on non-essential items is an emotional transaction, providing a fleeting dopamine hit of happiness that vanishes rapidly—compelling us to buy more and more things in an endless cycle.

Spending habits are often driven by the desire to align with a certain identity—the pressures of fitting in. In those instances, purchases may be more about projecting an image than fulfilling genuine needs.

Reflecting on my own experience in the corporate world—I was surrounded by people in designer clothes, bragging about exclusive restaurants and vacations. I later realised that my spending was a mask for my low self-worth and need to fit in.

Then there are the "Pretender Spenders"—people who showcase a "perfect life" through extravagant spending, yet behind the scenes they have very little wealth. I remember being a Pretender Spender in my twenties. I had a brand-new BMW, designer suit, and it appeared that "I'd made it." But in reality, I was in an entry level marketing job, I had credit card debt, car finance payments, and I spent every single pound of my earnings—with no savings in the bank. Living the western dream!

Contrary to popular belief, most of the millionaires I personally know don't dress in overtly expensive clothes. Instead they choose to invest, grow through personal development and have experiences with their loved ones instead. Many also donate their time to charitable work. Those last three also happen to be the most fulfilling of the 6 human needs: love and connection, growth and contribution.

In our journey toward environmental sustainability, financial freedom, and a simpler life, Sarah and I have embraced a reduction in our discretionary spending on "stuff"—**preferring experiences with our family and personal growth instead.**

Studies have proven that once your basic needs have been met, experiences bring more pleasure than material goods. **Outsourcing dissatisfiers to buy back your time, can also lead to more happiness.**

Discretionary spending **tends to silently grow as your earnings increase** and can make or break your financial journey. This is often termed "Lifestyle Inflation."

When you've covered your monthly essentials like the electricity bill, water, mortgage, and groceries—that's your essential living costs, or "needs." Now, *discretionary spending* is where those "wants" come in. It's those choices that shape your lifestyle and define your quality of life. Eating out, drinks with friends, a coffee to go, that gym membership, new clothes, holidays, the latest gadget—these are the things you choose to spend on because you want them. Mastering discretionary spending is about realising that none of these are real needs. You have the power to choose—not only to spend within your budget, but to have money left over to save and invest in your future every month.

Consider this: If Sarah and I receive a large bill, sometimes we will have a "no discretionary spend" month—every time we think about buying something, we remind ourselves of the rule we made for this month. Try it—you may be surprised at how much you can save in a month.

If you find yourself splurging every week, it's like having a weekly battle with your arch-nemesis, discretionary spending.

Similar to international opera singer Deanna Breiwick's thought process for deciding whether to buy something, **I also run through a mental gymnastics routine when considering a purchase**. See chapter 7 on relationships for Deanna's interview.

So, step into my mind palace, where I conduct a thorough interrogation before I even consider reaching for my wallet. Firstly, I ask myself **how long the happiness will last if I buy this item?** If it's just a minor upgrade—like getting the latest smartphone or a slightly newer version of your trusty old car—that bliss might evaporate in a few days. **But, if you're fixing a dissatisfying aspect of your life, then the happiness will stick around a lot longer.**

Then comes the big guns—value. **How much value will I get from this spend?** When it comes to books and courses, it can be a treasure trove of knowledge to improve your life, worth far more than the cost.

And, of course, we can't forget the environmental impact. **Am I contributing to the mountains of waste** due to unnecessary gadgets? Picture this: our kids have a clock and an Amazon Echo. Sarah was considering buying each of them a new Echo with a clock display to replace them—resulting in four perfectly good devices getting the boot. We eventually decided to wait until one of them breaks. In addition, we tend to buy electronic books, to save paper and have less clutter in our home.

So, before you open your wallet, challenge yourself: **Do you really "need" that item to survive, or is it a mere "want"?** Consider the value it provides, environmental impact, the financial cost, and the quest for a simpler, clutter-free life.

Evaluate Monthly Subscriptions

These are like these silent money ninjas. You've got TV, music, shopping, grocery delivery, clubs, days out, memberships, charity donations… it's like a subscription spending party.

I met an amazing mother facing imminent financial hardship. She only had a couple of months before the money from her divorce ran out, and she would be unable to pay the rent. After reviewing her bank statements, I discovered a huge chunk was dedicated to monthly charity subscriptions—of which there were so many. While each individual donation was modest, she seemed to be saying yes to every charity that crossed her mailbox, resulting in a significant amount every month.

While it's a really great thing to contribute to causes you're passionate about, make sure you don't donate so much that it adds to your financial difficulties.

So, before you sign up for another monthly subscription, take a minute to reflect. Close your eyes and envision the future you. Is that new subscription giving you joy or value? **And while you're at it, what about old subscriptions you barely use?** It's time to simplify!

Reduce the Cost of Your Home

This is where you spend a big chunk of your money. As people make more money, they often buy fancier and more expensive houses. But here's the thing—big houses cost more to take care of, contain more stuff, and take longer to clean. It's a lot of work and decisions.

And before you say it…talk about the pot calling the kettle black! Yes, I live in a reasonably large house at the moment, but **I'd like to at least suggest that downsizing is an option.** Sarah and I will look at all the options, including moving into an apartment when our kids eventually move out.

Also, think about how far your house is from your work. Commuting is never fun. Living closer can save you time and money.

If you work virtually, then consider the benefits of living in a cheaper area that you like—and is closer to your friends or family. Depending on how much cheaper it is, you might be able to sell your home and pay off your debts.

As we've worked from home for decades, we've made life simpler by moving closer to our parents. It's great because they not only help with babysitting but are also pretty handy with tools. As an added bonus, the area we moved to had slightly lower property prices than the previous one. If I wanted to move much further away in the UK, then it's possible to buy a house for half the cost of my current one.

But if you're looking to slash your home expenses even further…**we once met a family living year-round in a high-end caravan park**, just a short drive to the beach. Picture this: a large, three-bedroom, double width caravan worth a little over £100,000, complete with a huge open-plan kitchen lounge. It was fully connected to the mains. Backing onto a nature reserve, it gave them a front-row seat to nature and birdsong. Now, this park had a haven of amenities—a restaurant, bar, indoor swimming pool, crazy golf course, and activities ranging from roller skating to archery. Sarah and I spent a month seriously considering the idea of selling our home and diving headfirst into caravan park life. Alternatively, you can cut down the cost of caravan site fees by moving somewhere with no amenities.

Now, if you're interested in a romantic ideal, imagine living on a canal boat, navigating the waterways with your family. The enchantment of steering your boat to a new destination daily, breathing in the fresh air—it's an adventure. Yet, it comes with the trade-off of manually filling up your water and dealing with a cassette toilet. Privacy, especially if you have kids, is limited. I was concerned about keeping warm in the winter. However, when I visited a friend's boat, I was pleasantly surprised at how warm and cosy their log burner made their boat feel.

Alternatively, there's the allure of "van life." Whether it's a year-round residence in a campervan or a converted van, it's a lifestyle with even less privacy—ideal for solo warriors or couples seeking a nomadic existence. It gives you the freedom of embracing life on the open road.

Some of these options will seem like a large sacrifice, and others may pique your interest. **The point is to think outside the box, of ALL the potential options**, as there are many. Just moving to a smaller house or flat can drastically reduce your costs.

Reduce the Cost of Your Cars

In chapter three we talked about me selling my second car, because taking an occasional taxi was cheaper. With just one car, I only need to deal with one set of insurance and maintenance.

If you're in a city, you might not even need a car.

But if you do have one, keeping life simple is all about having a reliable car. I don't want the hassle of buying something cheap that breaks down all the time. No thanks! That's too many headaches.

LIVING A RICHER LIFE

Living a richer life, doesn't necessarily mean spending a lot of money. Each of us will have a different rich life. Rich might be walking your kids to and from school each day; learning a new language; having the time to volunteer for a charity; having the freedom to travel the country in a van; living abroad for a few months; or becoming debt-free.

Sometimes the simplest things give the greatest pleasures. In an interview on the Tim Ferris Show, Derek Sivers, founder of CD Baby recounted a day out with his son in London. He allowed his son to randomly turn from one street to the next, creating an exciting adventure. His son found some other kids to play with on one street.

Then later he found a large cardboard box and decided to poke some holes in it, so he could wear it around the city. Later they stopped outside a theatre where the next performance of Wicked the Musical was about to begin—so they bought some seats. At the end of the day when Derek was tucking his son into bed, he asked him, "What was the highlight of your day?" His son paused and thoughtfully said, "The cardboard box."

If you do have some money to spend, then look to your passions. What do you love to read about, watch, do, and talk about? Ramit Sethi suggests we ask, **"How can you use money to make that passion better?"**

That could encompass buying improved or additional equipment—providing you would realistically use it a lot. Alternatively, getting a personal lesson from an expert to enhance your skills, or visiting a specific place to soak up the atmosphere.

For example, when I wanted to improve my fitness, I took the Personal Trainer qualification. And when I went through the stressful events outlined in our story, I wanted to build myself a toolkit to better handle stress—so I took the yoga and meditation teaching qualifications. I wanted to improve my passions and my life.

From Savings to Fortune: The Art of Growing Your Wealth

WARNING: Whatever you decide to invest in, be aware that like all investments, your capital is at risk and the income and value of your fund can go up, as well as down. There is always risk. Speak with your Independent Financial Advisor before making any investments.

Your Net Worth is the total value of all your assets, including cash, minus loans.

If you only earn a paycheque and have no investments, then you will never achieve financial freedom and will always be working for someone else. The less work you have to do for the money, the more passive the income is.

Not only that, but if you have a desire to become wealthy, that will only come from investing in assets.

We've tracked our net worth for many years, to ensure we're still making progress.

Assets could be:

- Property (Real Estate)

- Stock Market

- Businesses

- Intellectual Property

- Other Asset Classes (such as gold, art, classic cars)

"When faced with complexity, the answer is simplicity."
—George Choy

If you look at top 100 rich lists around the world, you'll notice a common theme—most are investing their money in Property or the Stock Market. We will just look at the first two. They can both provide capital gains and income.

Seeing your wealth accumulate is sexy. But the process of getting rich is not sexy. It's just buying the same things over and over again and holding for the long term. Buy and forget. There's no need to reinvent the wheel—just follow the well-trodden path that the wealthy swear by.

So, stop working for time and build your money-making machine. Invest in your future self by buying assets to fund your early retirement. Once the income from these assets surpasses your personal expenses, you have the freedom to retire and pursue your passions.

Is it possible for anyone to become a millionaire—even if you don't have rich parents? Yes. **A survey by Fidelity Investments found that 86% of millionaires were self-made. They were not born wealthy.**[5]

I was in debt when I first met Sarah—but by the time she was 39 years old we were financially free. Neither of us had rich childhoods. We didn't win the lottery. What we had was total commitment to achieve financial freedom, above other goals. Most of that growth happened in only a couple of years. We've mentored students to achieve financial freedom in only 18 months. Five to ten years is achievable for most people, depending on your circumstances and how fully committed you are. Don't listen to the naysayers—you just need to start on the path and fully commit to it. It's also motivating to mix with people on the same path, or meeting people who've already achieved it.

If you would like to learn more about how to achieve financial freedom, please read one of our other books:
Stealth Millionaire: How to Save and Manage Your Money Like the Rich

Avoid High Risk Investments

Remember Warren Buffet's number one rule: don't lose money.

Some people are attracted to risky investments that wildly increase and decrease, because they think that's the quickest way to make more money. But that's not the case. Often, people lose everything.

The wealthy are extremely cautious about risk. **They focus on wealth preservation, and prefer modest and almost guaranteed growth, with very little downside.** That is because if your investment drops by 50%, you'll need to achieve 100% growth just to get back where you started.

A spokesman for one group of investors with over $100 million net worth commented that his members only allocated 1-3% of their wealth to risky investments. So, while investing £1-3 million on risky stuff sounds like a lot, it isn't relative to their portfolio.

You should also aim to diversify across asset classes as well as geography, to reduce your investing risks.

Property Investing

> *"Shop for houses not shoes."*
> —George Choy

One of the other qualities of Property investing (real estate) is that it is relatively stable, due to it being illiquid (i.e. slow to sell). When price declines happen, they are much slower than the stock market.

You can be the buy-and-hold landlord investor, or the much riskier property developer. **We mostly buy and hold for passive income.**

One great advantage of Property is the power of leverage. You can make your money work harder for you through use of mortgages—you might only need to put down a 25% deposit, depending on the ratio of rent to house value. Of course, you must calculate your numbers carefully, to ensure a good return on your investment.

Renting out properties is like hitting the jackpot twice. You get regular rent payments, plus your property can grow in value over time. On "average" in the UK, residential properties double every seven to nine years. There are fluctuations in appreciation and rental income between areas, so that is a key factor in your estimated returns. **One day Sarah and I had a lightbulb moment when we realised our home had increased more in one year than we'd earned in our jobs!**

Picture this: let's say you bought a property in the UK for £150,000. You took out a mortgage and only needed to put down £37,500 deposit.

Assuming you'd bought in a good location to achieve average growth, and the house doubled its value in nine years, then the house would now be valued at £300,000.

Your £37,500 cash deposit has now turned into £187,500 of equity.

You could choose to sell and keep the profit after taxes, or remortgage and take some of that equity out. In the meantime, you've also been receiving monthly rental income.

Let's imagine you'd got the investing bug and put down £150,000 deposit to buy £600,000 of houses.

If your properties doubled in nine years-time, they'd be worth £1.2 million.

Assuming you hadn't increased your loans, you'd now be a millionaire. That's just an illustration, as there's no guarantee that you will pick the right house, at the right price, in the right location, and that the market is up at the time, to achieve the average UK growth rate.

When it comes to renting—single-family homes are like magnets for tenants. There are often up to 25 people wanting to check out your property. There are just not enough houses to go around. Buying property might seem complicated, but **once you hand it over to a good letting agent, it becomes a pretty hands-off investment.**

Commercial property is whole other game. It can be more hands-off than residential property, because tenants often sign up for 5 or 10 years and pay for the maintenance. **However, it was a very steep learning curve** when we bought our first one, so it's not recommended for a first-time investor.

Now, Property Development doesn't tick the box of "passive income" or "simplifying." It's a boatload of work, stress, and comes with a lot of risk in return for potentially high rewards. If you're into managing projects, you might want to consider it, but it's probably better to tackle it after simplifying your life a bit.

In the meantime, you can consider lending to developers—we have done this in the past, and will no doubt do it again, as it can be fun and lucrative. **However, development is a high-risk strategy**, so make sure you have done full due diligence on the investor, proposed development, and have security in place in case the deal goes up in flames—which does happen from time to time. **Not every development is profitable.** And watch out for shady characters trying to get your money for properties they don't even own!

Stock Market Investing

The advantage of investing in the stock market is that you can invest a small amount each month—so it can be easier to get started here than in Property investing.

Check this out: **The S&P 500 returned 10.52% per year on average over the last 34 years.** Each year was higher, lower, or even negative returns, but the average was 10.52% annually over that period.[6]

SIMPLICITY SECRET

So, if you'd invested just $300 per month in the S&P 500 index at that rate of return, **you'd have become a millionaire after 34 years.** That shows the power of compounding returns over time.[7]

Many people consider day trading because they think they can beat the stock market. But don't do it! Remember, the number one rule to not lose money! It doesn't satisfy the simplicity rule, and finally, as billionaire hedge fund manager Ray Dalio said:

> *"But you can't do it by trying to beat the system.*
> *You don't want to try.*
> *I have fifteen hundred employees and forty years of*
> *experience, and it's a tough game for me.*
> *This is poker with the best poker players on earth."*
> —Ray Dalio

Plus, here's a mind-blowing fact: **about 80% of professional fund managers don't outperform a simple index fund like the S&P 500.**[8]

The advantage of an index fund like the S&P 500, is that as companies become more successful, they automatically rise in the index and the poor performers drop out. **So, you don't need to pick individual stocks, as you will always be tracking the best.** You also have a broad diversification of companies, not limited to a specific sector. **In addition, fund managers may charge ten times more in fees than a low-cost index fund.**

Even Warren Buffett, the billionaire investor, suggests putting your money in a low-cost index fund like the S&P 500.

Moreover, you don't have to exhaust your decision-bank. **Use the *Habitualise Your Savings* method to set up automatic transfers from your bank, to a specific index fund every month.** It's called "dollar cost averaging," as it smooths out the highs and lows in your investment journey. Aim to buy and hold your investments for at least 10 years.

But what about bonds? They have less ups and downs than stocks, but the returns are usually lower. People often suggest to have more bonds as you get closer to retirement age.

However, Warren Buffet recommends allocating 90% to a low-cost index fund and 10% to short-term government bonds.

Alternatively, Billionaire Fund Manager, Ray Dalio recommends using an *All Weather Portfolio*:

30% Index funds
40% Long term treasury bonds
15% Intermediate term treasury bonds
7.5% Commodities
7.5% Gold

Also consider leveraging tax-efficient wrappers to house your stocks and shares. That entails placing your investments within products like ISAs in the UK, where all the earnings remain untaxed. It's a savvy move that optimizes your financial situation by minimizing the impact of taxes.

Investing in the stock market should be for the long term. There will be ups and downs. Make sure to look at the index fund chart for the last 50 years, to reassure yourself that you don't need to sell the next time the market dips—that's when the market is on sale and the wealthy often buy more!

Speak with a qualified financial professional and tax advisor before making your investing decisions.

Review Your Assets

We like to review our assets at least once a year to decide whether to buy more or sell and redistribute to a different asset class. We usually buy assets with the aim to hold for at least five years, if not forever.

Three things we consider: Performance, Annoyance and Strategy.

1. Performance: does the real return still fit your requirements, or is there scope to improve it in the future? Be wary of selling in a market downturn.

2. Annoyance: sometimes an asset performs well financially but is a complete pain in the ass! For instance, perhaps you own a property in a deprived area that consistently attracts anti-social behaviour. Maybe it's time to substitute it for a property in a better area, to get rid of the headache.

3. Strategy: occasionally the asset is great, but you want to pursue a different strategy now. For instance, we're selling two properties to fund the build of our new home.

STRESS-FREE RETIREMENT

PENSIONS

If you're anything like us, then you've worked in multiple companies and have more than one pension. **In the UK it may be possible to transfer the funds and consolidate them.** But there can be exceptions if: one of your pensions is worth over £30,000; if they are defined benefit pensions; or if they are provided by a government department. Pensions are highly regulated—this is one area where it is **often a legal requirement in the UK to seek the advice of an Independent Financial Advisor (IFA).**

Sarah and I wanted to have more control over our pensions, so we opted to set up a Small Self-Administered Scheme (SSAS). It allows up to eleven members within the same fund, so we could eventually include our children when they become adults. We can choose how to invest the funds and lend a proportion back to our company if we wish to. We can even buy commercial property with it. It's a company pension, so you can only set up a SSAS if you own a limited company. We moved four pension pots into one account to simplify our pensions.

If you're single, or your partner does not wish to pool their pension funds with yours, and you still want to control what your funds are invested in, then an alternative UK product is a Self-Invested Personal Pension (SIPP). This product has more limitations than a SSAS on what you can invest in, and it does not permit loans to your company.

If you don't want the responsibility of controlling your pension, then you may be able to transfer your pension pots into one of your existing pensions. You must seek advice of an Independent Financial Advisor.

Retirement Planning

I frequently meet people who are just five or ten years away from retirement, and let me tell you, many of them are in a state of panic. They're wondering if their pension is enough to retire comfortably.

Now, the first thing you need to do, is to take a couple of deep breaths. Then, open a spreadsheet or a grab a piece of paper, and let's get down to business—**calculate exactly how much money you'll be receiving from different sources, including when they will be hitting your bank account.** Include state and private pensions, money from investments and anything else that has regular income.

Secondly, calculate your current household spend, then project into the future and remove work related expenses such as commuting. Perhaps your children will have left home, so you won't need such a large house anymore.

If you've got it all covered, fantastic! But if there's a bit of a shortage, then it's time to simplify. **Consider streamlining your life to close that gap.** Alternatively, think about what kind of part-time work you could take on after you reach retirement age. **Maybe even turn that passion project of yours into a part-time business.** The possibilities are endless when it comes to securing your financial future.

Advanced Planning: If I Die

A lot of people don't plan for the inevitable. But not us. When Sarah and I were in our twenties we already had a will and were planning for our future.

One of my friends is an Estate Planner. You would not believe the mess and fighting amongst relations that occurs when you don't have an up-to-date will. If you have any assets at all, or have kids, then you really should have a will. Although preparing doesn't simplify your life right now, it will give you the peace of mind knowing that the right people will inherit your legacy when you pass on.

Not only that, but with dementia on the rise, and the possibility of being involved in an unpredictable accident, there's no guarantee you will be in a sensible mental state to manage your finances. **Sarah and I both have a *Lasting Power of Attorney* to manage each other's financial and health affairs, should we become incapacitated.** It's wise to arrange it while you are still in good health.

We created a document we aptly named "If I die." The Executors of our Will have a copy of this. It outlines what we own, what investments we have, and other essential information the Executor of our will need to finalise our estate. It takes a bit of effort to create, but it's a gift to whoever sorts out your affairs.

To make it easy for you, we've included our *If I Die* template in the Bonus Content area of Chapter 2:
bit.ly/ss-bonus-content

Next we'll hear from Diana Finch-Keran on how her life turned upside down—forcing her to leave corporate life and simplify her finances.

Interview: Diana Finch-Keran, UK Yoga Teacher

What was your life like as the breadwinner for your family?

I have always been career-driven and this is from my culture, from my upbringing in Romania. They push you to get higher education, to be successful in your job, and to buy material things as a status symbol. I had a strong drive to succeed—wanting to get to the top. It wasn't about titles; I just wanted to serve at a really high level. I worked relentlessly for twenty-two years—I did not stop. I couldn't honestly call my holidays, a holiday. I appeared successful on the outside—very good if we're talking about salary. I didn't worry about my expenditure.

What changed for you?

It started abruptly with my husband's poor health, which shocked me, because he couldn't walk anymore, and he couldn't work. I was busy working all hours in a company that had six different companies underneath it. And as much as I loved to do everything, there was so much going on in my home life.

It got overwhelming—I had no time to be a mum, or a wife. My husband lost his health and confidence, because he couldn't provide money for our family—which for some reason, society makes you feel you're not good enough.

Then after two years of battling with his health, I started struggling with my mental health. I didn't recognise it at first, because in the culture I come from, you have to be strong—you have to keep working hard.

I was working all hours of the day. I'd drive my fourteen-year-old son to school in morning, and almost push him out of the car so I could rush to work. Later, I'd run to the office, go pick him up from school, catapult him home and then rush back to the office to continue working. I rarely spent time with him at the weekend as I was always working. I felt so tired and stressed out all the time. I was often angry coming home—nothing was good enough. Even insignificant things would set me off, like the fork being out of place, stains on the furniture and things like that.

I was so desperate to help my husband get his life back that we started paying for him to have operations abroad. For three years we spent tens of thousands of pounds. I didn't mind spending the money. I just wanted him back. I worked harder than ever.

One day we reached a melting point in our family, and everything turned black. I was sitting down with my husband and son—I breathe through my son, he's quite a wise little man. My son said something that really woke me up. He said, "You are a workaholic monster."

That hit me hard. I cried. He said, "You have to leave your job." And that's where life stopped. I had mixed emotions as I my entire life revolved around my job. I was working to bring financial stability to my family.

I started justifying my work. "I need to work because I can take you on expensive holidays. I can buy you brand new uniforms costing £600 in one go without blinking, because I want you to have the best." Those expensive habits had grown over time as my income went up. I said to him that I would think about it.

My son labelling me a "workaholic monster" hit me really deep in my heart and sounded so true. A week later, I handed in my resignation.

How did you simplify your finances after leaving such a highly paid job?

I didn't want another job. I wanted some time to myself to recalibrate—to become a mum and wife again. I thought I'd give myself three months.

I'd gone from a six-figure salary to nothing. I asked myself how we were going to manage financially, because my savings would eventually run out. I like to be organised, so I put plans in place.

Plans on how we eat, what we do at home, what we do when we go out. I know it sounds controlling, but the three of us sit down at the table to discuss these things—they are my council.

We had conversations like "Why do we want to go out? Why do we want to go to that restaurant? Why do we have to go out three times a week?" We came to the conclusion that we were really looking for time together as a family. We've moved towards more conscious living, spending and gifting.

I'd been practicing yoga for over fifteen years. So, after I quit my job, I studied for the yoga teacher qualification and started holding yoga classes where I live in Essex. I love to feel my student's energy. I like to offer people more than a yoga class; it's an experience.

Recently my son asked me, "What do you want for your birthday, Christmas and name day?" Previously I'd said I wanted a Tesla car. But I'm not so interested in material things now—we prefer experiences. So, I said I wanted to extend my Happy Jack Yoga membership for another year instead. Now I'm sorted for another year. I don't need presents.

Experiences don't need to cost a lot of money. It can be anything small like going for a walk together or spending an hour to watch a comedy. We also have our family reading club first thing in the morning, and also before we go to sleep—we lie down on the bed like three sausages and we read books together.

How has your life changed?

When I was in corporate life, I got to a point where I hated Monday's—when you wake up feeling anxiety building up in your chest and your stomach. I wasn't getting enough sleep. I'd come home from the office, skip dinner, have a shower and throw myself in bed. I'd sleep for twelve hours. I think I just wanted to numb myself, because of how unhappy I was—it was some sort of depression. Blocking it through sleep felt like a safe place to me.

Nowadays I wake up really early at 4.30 in the morning, excited about whatever the day brings. My outlook on life has completely changed. Sometimes bad things happen, and I make them really good. My son always smiles when I tell him stories of bad things that have happened—he asks, "How can you laugh about this?" I have a positive mindset now.

Recently a friend of mine contacted me about a corporate job in London, for a different company. I brought it up at our family council meeting, and with without hesitation, they both said, absolutely not. They said they didn't want the old person to come back in this house. That was that good for me to hear, because that meant that they sensed and felt the changes I'd made.

FOLLOW DIANA FINCH-KERAN:

Website: linktr.ee/yogadianakeran

Facebook: @holisticdianakeran
Instagram: @holisticdianakeran

Conclusion: Money

The journey towards financial security begins with the art of habitual saving and strategic investing. Take a closer look at your home and cars—evaluate them against your long-term financial goals. Plan your legacy, no matter how young you are.

Streamline your finances and let go of unnecessary complexities. Become aware of your discretionary spending—ask yourself whether it provides value or lasting joy.

Embrace the philosophy that simplicity is often the quickest path to financial success—take the well-trodden path of the wealthy. There's no need to reinvent the wheel.

By decluttering and simplifying your financial landscape, you'll pave the way for financial stability and prosperity.

CHAPTER 6

Enjoy Your Work and Mission

"Complexity is your enemy.
Any fool can make something complicated
It is hard to keep things simple."
— Sir Richard Branson

Get ready to unleash ultimate job satisfaction, become a productivity superhero, and streamline your business like a pro.

But wait, there's more! **We've got an exclusive interview with the inspirational Sarah Beth of Sarah Beth Yoga**, spilling the beans on how she simplified her life, improved her mental health and grew a 7-figure business through the magical art of delegation. This section is your one-stop-shop for career enlightenment, productivity hacks, and the secrets to a simplified business journey!

My wife and I have been at the helm of our own primary business or a side hustle for twenty years. I spent almost two decades working in corporate marketing and general management. I could go on about this topic indefinitely, but I've made an effort to distil the main issues I consistently hear from the people I speak with.

As you evaluate your business or mission, keep the Simplicity Secret Tool in mind:

D Delete   **O** Outsource   **S** Substitute   **H** Habitulise

↓

AND THEN WHAT?

SIMPLICITY SECRET

Will you bid farewell to your 9-5 job by *deleting* it?

Will you *outsource* tasks in your business, *substitute* tools or personnel with superior ones, or streamline tasks through *habitual* automation?

And then what will the future outcome look like as you play it through in your mind? The choice is yours.

ARE YOU IN THE RIGHT JOB?

According to research carried out by Indeed, 71% of workers are unhappy with their job.[9] They measured it in terms of workers happiness, purpose, stress and satisfaction.

Some of the lowest points in my life were either doing work that was unfulfilling or working with people who acted unethically. This resulted in constant stress and depression. I should have left sooner, but I didn't have the courage at the time. However, overcoming these low points has positively transformed my life in ways I could never have imagined.

With most people being unsatisfied in their jobs, the question is why they are still working there, when there will always be other jobs paying a similar amount of money?

Imagine this: You put your nose to the grindstone until you're 65, for two vacations a year. You "hope" that your pension will be enough. And then, maybe, you get a shot at enjoying 20 years of perfect health doing what you love. Doesn't make sense, right?

Why wait to enjoy life? Live your life now!

If you spend most of your day working, why let most of your day be a downer?

Is the commute a drag? A University of Zurich study cited that people wanted a 40% pay raise to offset the misery of a one-hour commute to work.[10]

Do you feel like your authentic self at work? Or do you have to be a different person in order to perform your job well? Inauthenticity drains you over time.

Are you doing what you want to do, or are you living your parent's life out of obligation? I have a doctor friend who owns a private clinic. Each of his children felt obliged to study medicine to become a doctor. The question is, are they living their true life?

But what work should you do? We've drummed it into our kids—it's not about the cash, it's about loving what you do and the people you're working with. **If your passionate about your work, you can excel—and people will pay more for it.**

The key to unlocking a professional life that harmonises with your best-self, is to be crystal clear about your values, passions, and purpose.

What truly lights a fire within you?

What ignites a spark of excitement every morning?

Moreover, your work ideally would also contribute to the world. How does it serve others? How does it contribute to a greater cause? This alignment with a higher purpose gives your work meaning and fuels the passion that propels you towards your best life.

Contribution is the main reason we felt compelled to write Simplicity Secret. We wanted to help people going through tough times and help them become stronger for the future.

Here's a thought experiment: picture winning £2 million tomorrow, or whatever amount would completely erase your financial worries.

Sure, you might indulge in relaxation and travelling all over the world, but what comes after? Most of us have a desire to contribute meaningfully to the world—to be useful. What would you choose to do?

Would you devote more time to your artistic pursuits, perhaps showcasing your paintings in an exhibition?

How about finally realizing that dream of becoming a yoga teacher, or sharing your experiences by writing a book?

Could you venture into a new field, completely shifting careers to pursue something more fulfilling?

Maybe you'd explore the globe, capturing breath-taking photos to share your inspiring journey with others in a blog.

The possibilities are boundless and uniquely yours.

So, what's stopping you from pursuing those dreams right now?

I once met a woman who aspired to join Doctors Without Borders. Despite her burning passion, she was stuck in her job, merely counting down the days until her retirement. With her daughter already moved out, living alone, I asked her, "Why not rent out your home and pursue your dream now?" There was truly nothing preventing her from living her dream immediately, instead of postponing it for another 15 years.

What about you? Could you live your dream right now?

If you're not in a position to quit your job immediately, how can you move towards your dream?

What are you doing in your current role that is preparing you for your next chapter?

Could you tweak your job to make it more satisfying by changing what you do, day-to-day?

Is transitioning to a new job an option? One that offers the necessary learning experiences for free, or even pays for your training?

Take Sarah, for example, who worked at a lettings and estate agency for a few years, to gain valuable experience in property management. She was essentially getting paid to learn, and those skills have paid off handsomely over the past two decades.

> *"There is no greater thing you can do with your life and your work than follow your passions – in a way that serves the world and you."*
> — Sir Richard Branson

If you're stuck at a crossroads, unsure about your life's direction, check out one of our other books:

Find Your Purpose: A Practical Guide for Discovering Your Purpose and Creating a Life You Love
bit.ly/fypurpose

Changing jobs or careers can be challenging, as our personal identity is often closely connected to our work.

In *Find Your Purpose*, an entire chapter is devoted to the concept of Identity. However, a simple and effective strategy is to experiment with different identities, by declaring "I am a..." Try on various roles until you discover one that resonates with you, and then consistently repeat it until it naturally becomes your response.

YOU'RE GETTING PAID EVEN LESS THAN YOU THINK!

One way to transform the way you view your current job, is to **take a deep dive into the hidden costs of working.**

Back in my corporate days, it took me a long time to realise there was a whole symphony of expenditures playing in the background.

Start with the basics. Factor in the cost of parking at the station, the fuel from your commute, the annual depreciation of your car, those seemingly innocent lunch outings with colleagues, the dry-cleaning bills, childcare, and the subtle pressure to flaunt designer clothes. Now, that's just the tip of the iceberg.

Now, brace yourself as you subtract all those hidden costs. You might be left wondering if chasing your passion from the comfort of your own home could bring the same, if not better, cash flow.

We've guided many of our previous mentees through this transformative exercise, and the outcomes have been astounding. Picture the moment of revelation when some of our mentees discovered the possibility of retiring within 18-months. It's an eye-opener.

You might uncover that you only need a fraction of your current income to live your dream life. Or, you could be bleeding money by showing up to that 9-to-5 job. If that's the case, it's time to take charge. Ask for that raise you deserve, cut your hours, demand to work from home, or if it's time to make a change, take the courageous step to resign.

Remember, your decisions lead to your destiny, and it's time to rewrite the script for abundance and fulfilment!

If you really want to blow your mind—divide your monthly income by the number of hours you spend working, commuting and travelling for work.

You might find that after deducting all costs you would get paid more in a local, unskilled job—and have a lot less stress.

In one of my previous corporate jobs, I travelled abroad for work every fortnight—usually leaving on Sunday afternoon. That sounds glamourous, but my enthusiasm for travelling wore out fast! I regularly took conference calls during my holidays too. I was so tired all the time. If I'd worked out how much I was really earning per hour, I might have discovered that I was only working for minimum wage.

GETTING SHIT DONE!

I wasn't always a highly productive action-taker. Until my early-twenties, I was late for nearly everything! It has taken me many years to hone this skill into a driving force for massive results! Now it's one of my biggest strengths. Let's look through the easy ways you can increase your productivity.

SET BIG DOMINO GOALS

Sarah and I consistently set a couple of monumental business goals each year, reviewing them weekly. These domino goals can have life-changing effects.

We channel our time and energy into progressing these goals, moving them to the next stage, day-by-day. Every step is a win. This deliberate approach guarantees that we focus on what truly matters, aligning our actions with our highest priorities.

Stop the Busywork

Often, we are simply creating busywork and not progressing our big goals. For example, I remember once when I was tracking so many statistics from marketing campaigns and social media, that eventually I realised that I was just compiling stats for the sake of it.

Sure, it felt reassuring to have all these results at my fingertips, but did they really count? At the end of the day, what was more important was whether a communication resulted in a sale? If not, then would my time be better suited to sending out another communication with free content to build engagement, instead of getting lost in endless analysis. And let's not forget decision fatigue—all the time spent on busywork is impacting growing your business.

Now, I'm not saying don't track anything. You obviously need to do your bookkeeping to record your company accounts. **And there are key metrics like your company or small business revenue, sales, expenses and profitability that you should definitely track and review each month.** Otherwise, before long, you could be out of business. There are many more statistics you could track, such as the size of your email list, retention statistics and much more. All I'm suggesting is that you stick to those metrics where you will actually take action on the information. **If it's just for info, then use your valuable time for something else!**

Remember: When faced with complexity, the answer is simplicity.

As you review the tasks you were planning to do today, reflect upon whether your time will move the needle, or if you need to focus on something else.

Stop Multi-Tasking at Work

One productivity illusion is multi-tasking. You've probably seen people on conference or video calls, checking emails and social media at the same time. On the surface they may look more productive, but in reality, the brain is constantly switching between activities and reducing concentration. A study by Wagner, a professor of psychology at Stanford University, found that, **heavier media multitaskers often exhibited poorer performance**.[11]

SAY NO TO MEETINGS

When I worked in the corporate world, I attended meeting after meeting, and found it hard to get anything done. I often wondered why I was there? I was too polite to turn them down.

Entrepreneur and investor Naval Ravikant once tweeted: **"You should be too busy to do coffee, while still keeping an uncluttered calendar."** He lives by that rule and doesn't do meetings unless there is a transaction taking place.

The question to ask yourself is: "if I accept this coffee meeting, will it be fair exchange?" Dr John Demartini says "In every transaction, both individuals keep an inventory of what has been given and what has been taken."

For industry experts offering paid mentoring sessions, a casual coffee or lunch invitation would not reflect the true value of their time and expertise.

Because I receive a ton of requests every day for "a quick chat for some advice," I've had to make a rule of charging for all advice chats and mentoring, as they take time. We are happy to do it, but we need fair exchange.

However, doing things for your kids and parents is motivated by love and care, establishing a different kind of balance, based on emotional connection and support.

In the world of business, fair exchange can be observed when people accept interviews or speaking engagements to showcase their products or services—both sides receive immense value.

On a different note, in the past, I've been a sucker for saying 'yes' to meetings outside of my comfortable working hours. For example, when I was a Personal Trainer, I accepted clients in the evening. That might have been good for them as night owls, but as I get up at 5am, the evening sessions were too close to my bedtime. I was sacrificing restful sleep, just to make more money.

And when I was in the corporate world, I'd be on stressful conference calls during my vacations. I remember standing at summit of Mount Etna in Sicily engaged in a conference call, while Sarah was enjoying the scenery.

Fast forward to today, where Sarah and I have mastered the art of **work-life integration, rather than work-life balance**. There are no meetings after 5 pm, allowing us to enjoy quality moments with our kids. Moreover, recognizing the power of peak performance, we aim to wrap up most work by 2 pm.

What we call "work," also encompasses managing our house. It includes things like renewing insurance, ordering groceries and doing household chores. We don't stick to typical working days of the week, preferring instead to optimise around our home life. We have our date day during the week, as it is quieter when we go on trips.

Here's the golden rule: Your work should never overpower your home life.

The next time you're beckoned to a meeting, assess its fairness, evaluate your personal interest, and set clear boundaries on the times you're available. Your time is valuable, and investing it wisely ensures not only professional success, but a thriving, balanced life.

BE GOOD ENOUGH

As a recovering "perfectionist," I used to invest a huge amount of time refining reports, web pages, and various projects, continually chasing a level of perfection that was never attainable.

The concept of Parkinson's Law, states that work expands to fill the time allotted. If I allocated two weeks for a task, I'd spend the entire time working on it—and often, double that amount.

The best choice is usually the simplest one. That reminds me of the time I recorded a short portrait style video on my phone, to upload to social media. Great simple choice so far, as I didn't need to turn on my studio setup. I was happy with the video, but it was thirty seconds over the one-minute limit. My first thought was, no problem, I'll import it into my video editing program, chop out some of the pauses, and maybe speed up part of it. Should take me twenty minutes. Sarah laughed and said it would be quicker to record it again—but talk faster!

Another example of choosing the path of simplicity occurred in my weekly vlog. For a couple of years, I'd been uploading videos to YouTube, then embedding them into a new page on my website. It wasn't a quick process. One day, Sarah came up with the idea to stop posting on my website and just direct everyone to YouTube. I remember feeling really nervous as I selected over 300 web pages…and paused with my finger over the delete key! However, once I had done that, it saved me a ton of time each week. Simple is faster.

Nowadays, I ask myself the question: "Is it good enough?"

This simple question has granted me the freedom to shed my unrealistic standards, allowing me to produce work that is suitable for the task, and increase my productivity. It has become a source of liberation, enabling me to break free from the chains of perfectionism.

Occasionally, I'm still tempted to endlessly tinker with things. However, in those moments, Sarah gives a guiding reminder, to redirect my energy towards our big goals.

Your Golden Productive Hours

There will be times of the day when you know you are usually the most productive, the most alert, you are on fire!

Night owls might reach their productivity peak in the afternoon or evening—but not for *larks* like us.

We rise early at 5 am and spend two hours nourishing ourselves with a self-care routine—more on self-care in chapter on tools to reduce stress. Our nurture-time helps us to build our emotional strength, before our kids get up and our "work" day begins.

Then at 9am we do the "frog tasks"—those tasks you would rather not do and tend to move from week to week.

Following this, we focus on anything that requires a lot of thought—like progressing domino goals, analysing numbers in a spreadsheet, managing money, or writing a book.

Remember: the quality of your decisions goes down as the day progresses—so we arrange most of our meetings for the early afternoon, when we don't need to concentrate as much. By 2pm we feel like our brain is fried, so we usually just relax.

Let's enhance this by delving into the powerful concept of "chunking"—dedicating a substantial block of time to a single task, while shutting out distractions.

It can take about twenty minutes to truly immerse yourself in a task, so if you only allocate half an hour, you might feel like you've barely scratched the surface. So, the next time you're faced with the challenge of crafting a report, or some other substantial task, you might consider dedicating an entire day to it, instead of splitting it across the week.

Remember, concentration goes down when you multi-task. So, shutting off distractions like your phone and email increases your focus, transforming sporadic hours into a powerhouse of productivity.

Every now and then, I engage in tasks demanding intense concentration, to the extent that after just an hour, I feel wiped out! In those moments, I shift all my to-do items to the next day or focus on minor chores that don't require much brain power. I'm aware that mistakes will be made if I don't do that.

So, give some thought to optimising the structure of your day, to ensure you tackle the most crucial tasks when your productivity and alertness are at their peak. It's about structuring your day for ultimate impact and success!

BATTLING THE EMAIL MONSTER

I recently saw a friend proudly declaring that she had 1,111 unopened emails! Sorry Sue!

Just thinking about a red notification icon with those high digits raises my stress levels, and it's not even my inbox! I can only imagine the epic battle she is facing against that mountain of emails. But fear not, brave email warrior, for with a few quirky rules, you can conquer the email monster and emerge victorious!

The first step is to stop the onslaught before it begins. **Keep your email address incognito, hidden away from the prying eyes of spam bots.** Encourage people to reach out via social media, or a contact form on your website with spam-bot protection.

Now, I do subscribe to my favourite people and industry updates, as it's a great way to curate content. **But if they're not sparking joy or fuelling my passions, then I hit the unsubscribe link.**

I don't just press delete and hope for the best; they'll keep coming back every week with reinforcements. Don't forget, if they email once a week, then that's 52 more emails to delete, instead of a little short-term pain to click unsubscribe.

Back to the warrior with 1,111 emails. As you can see from the math, it only takes 21 people to email you once a week, to reach over 1,000 emails a year. But fear not, an unsubscribe spree awaits you!

Simply open one email and unsubscribe, then search for all emails with the same sender address. You'll be able to quickly check the contents of each one, before hitting the delete key. Your inbox will be cleansed. Cue the music.

If you're not sure how to search, then **perhaps every time you make yourself a drink or visit the bathroom, you challenge yourself to unsubscribe and delete three emails.**

Let me share with you my simple rules for managing my email inbox. **I aim to have only a handful of emails in my inbox—these are orders or bookings that haven't arrived yet.** For example, in my inbox today is a booking for a restaurant, booking for my car service, and a coffee shop e-gift card that I need to show when I make a purchase.

I move emails that I need to keep to an archive folder and delete the rest, leaving a pristine inbox. Now, go forth and tame that unruly email monster!

BUSINESS PRODUCTIVITY TOOLS

Welcome to the wacky world of Business Productivity Tools.

In the awesome Bonus Content area of Chapter 2, we've included links to business tools that we currently use or have used and still highly recommend. And guess what? I've also got links to special offers and free trials where available.
bit.ly/ss-bonus-content

Our specific recommendations may change over time, so I'll list actual suppliers in the bonus content and only give general recommendations here.

Cloud Storage

Let's talk about going digital with Cloud Storage, the superhero that could have rescued my friend from the tragic death of her laptop!

Cloud storage was such a gamechanger for us. As tax returns for small businesses started going digital, we decided to shred the entire contents of our large three-drawer filing cabinet, and only scan in what was essential. It looked like a mammoth task, so we did it in bitesize chunks for an hour a day over a month. We were left with a single, humble folder for things like birth certificates and passports.

Sarah and I share the same cloud space—accessible from anywhere on Earth, thanks to the magic of laptops and phones. We even synchronized our Notes and Calendar, making us the Superman and Wonder Woman of digital organisation.

Our iPhones and iPads also allow us to back up our devices to Apple iCloud. This means that in the event our phones are broken, lost, stolen, or we buy a new one, it's easy to transfer all of our data and settings to a new phone, saving a lot of time during the setup process.

Email List

Your email list is the lifeblood of your business. I recommend you chose a supplier that provides both email marketing and landing pages for email opt-ins. It's easy to import a file with your email list to a new provider.

However, if you're hosting online courses, then it may be more cost-effective and less complex to use an integrated platform that combines courses, landing pages and email marketing.

I've listed my specific recommendations for both options in the bonus content area.

Taking Payment

You've got to make a living, so this is a must. There are many providers to choose from. A useful tip is to make sure the payment provider integrates with your other platforms.

Website domain registration and hosting

You don't necessarily need a website. These days you can easily build a business with one social media channel, an email marketing provider, and payment provider. You could be making your first sale within a day!

However, what I would say, is that it's really useful to register a URL or website domain name, so you can have a unique email address. That looks a lot more professional than a free email address. You can choose to redirect your website to a free menu-based landing page, or social media page, if you don't want the hassle of designing a website. Just choose a name that's easy for a 7-year-old to spell, to make it simple for people to type into web browsers.

Video Meetings

These have been the unsung hero of the pandemic. No more travelling to meetings.

You can use it for meetings, webinars, live training courses and even having a relaxing social evening with your friends across the globe. It's also useful to record videos for any courses you create, or to transcribe meetings.

MAKING BUSINESS SIMPLE

Most of the people I know have a business or want to start one as a side hustle. This sounds very grand, but often it's comprised of just one or two people. Here are a few questions people ask me time and time again.

THE UNIVERSE LOVES SPEED

When you have an inspiring idea, test it out before going into full production. This process is known as **creating the Minimum Viable Product (MVP)**. It will prevent you from wasting time on products that nobody wants. **Moreover, you'll end up with an even better product by listening to your audience.**

You could discuss the theme of your product through video calls, surveys, or social media groups. Collate their issues and outline a concept to solve the problem.

For instance, after we started simplifying our life, I noticed that nearly everyone mentioned the need to simplify their life, in calls we went on. So, I already knew there was a level of interest. As I started sharing some of the steps we had taken, there was a lot of engagement.

Sarah wanted us to write a book about simplicity. I found the topic really inspiring, as it had helped us so much. On the one hand, I was reluctant to take on another project at the time, as I didn't want to put us over the edge again. On the other hand, we felt we didn't really have a choice, as so many of our friends were suffering and desperately needed this information. So here we are.

Subsequently, I sent out a survey asking people about which areas of their life they needed to simplify. I then aimed to address as many of their issues as possible in the 'Simplicity Secret' book you are reading right now. I've also taken similar steps to create courses and events in the past.

If you wanted to take it up a level, you could then put together a framework with their themes and discuss it with your audience.

Alternatively, create a very rough prototype. Mark Zuckerberg created the prototype version of Facebook in just one night, with the aim of connecting Harvard students with each other. By the next day, over a thousand people had registered. That showed there was very high interest. Facebook now has over 3 billion monthly active users.

You can take it even further by asking people to register their interest in your product or service—or even better, ask them to buy it or put down a reservation fee. For example, Tesla asked for a $100 deposit to pre-order their Cybertruck and received over 250,000 reservations within a week.

You could also consider pre-selling a live training event. If people buy tickets, then go ahead and create the training slides. If nobody buys, then you haven't wasted your time.

WHAT TO DO WHEN IT ALL GOES WRONG

Life isn't perfect. Things will go wrong. No doubt you've already read our story and the pain we suffered in Chapter 1.

I also remember one time as a PT, when I opened up an exercise class and nobody turned up. Oh, and who could forget the epic webinar, where I spoke for 20 minutes before I realised that my microphone was on mute.

When something goes wrong and you really don't know which way to turn, **it's useful to have someone to talk it through with**. Sarah is not only my wife, but also my business partner—so we navigate the chaos together.

If it's a question more suited to our power team, then we ask them.

We also have our mentors to ask. I highly recommend paying for a good mentor—these are your superheroes. They can compress decades of wisdom into days.

The main thing about mistakes and failures, is learning from them—not beating yourself up and improving next time.

Choosing Your Company Name

The age-old quest for the perfect company name—more challenging than a sudoku puzzle! This one nemesis stops more businesses from being started than I can count. I often meet aspiring entrepreneurs who feel they can't kickstart their side-hustle until they've discovered the "perfect" name. **It becomes a barrier to getting started and earning money.**

If you have a small one or two-person business and you're the lead face and provider of the service, then your clients might not even remember the name of your business—we learned this the hard way when we ran a property investing and financial freedom training company. Despite our meticulously crafted company name and logo, most people just knew us as Sarah and George. I mean, what's the point of spending all those hours coming up with a company name when clients can't even remember it?

Sometimes, your own name is all you need. For example, Tony Robbins. Other times it can be useful to add a descriptive word after your name, so that people know what you are offering. Great examples are Happy Jack Yoga, Sarah Beth Yoga and The Tim Ferriss Show.

The exception to this is when you are not selling yourself as the main act but are selling your team or products. In those cases, crafting a memorable name is essential, especially if you're dreaming of selling your empire one day.

Your name builds reputation. Many famous product focused brands are simply the surname of the founder: Armani, Chanel, Cadbury, Dior, Disney, Bloomberg, Dell, Chevrolet, Ford.

Company Structure

Prior to setting up a company, it's prudent to seek the advice of an Accountant and Tax professional. Clearly outline your objectives and requirements, asking them to take into account your personal circumstances.

If your industry requires specialist knowledge, such as property investing, then it's worthwhile finding a good accountant that specialises in that area. Switching accountant is not easy, so it is useful to take your time choosing. Ask your friends whether they are happy with their accountant. Be very cautious of any accountants offering schemes that seem too good to be true, when other accountants don't feel it is advisable to take that route.

Company structures can be intricate, involving elements like varied shares and ownership configurations, and also op-co prop-co models where the operational company (op-co) leases from the property company (prop-co).

However, before diving into a complicated structure, consider whether you should set up a company in the first place. Each company incurs costs, such as accounting fees, bank account charges, and company registration expenses. If your operations are on a smaller scale in the UK, then alternatives like registering as a Sole Trader or Partnership might be simpler and still meet your needs.

For those already managing multiple companies, like us, you might consider closing some. As highlighted in our story, we've made strategic decision to close one company and are currently in the process of shutting another—in an effort aimed at simplifying our lives and concentrating on our key priorities. Every company you add entails more fees, more banks, more documentation and reporting. **And let's not forget, every additional company adds to decision fatigue.**

WEARING MANY HATS

If you're a solo entrepreneur, then unfortunately you're juggling all the elements in your business. You are the managing director, head of marketing and sales, head of human resources, head of technology, bookkeeper—the list goes on and on.

Luckily, Sarah and I are also business partners, so we can share the load. **Years ago, we sat down to identify the tasks we are really good at, enjoy, or dislike—then we allocated our responsibilities.** In cases where both of us are equally involved, we always assign one of us to take the lead role interacting with suppliers—otherwise it causes a lot of confusion for them.

USE YOUR POWER TEAM

If you are regularly paying Mentors, Accountants, Tax Advisors, Pension companies and Lawyers for advice, then use them! It's much more effective to get the correct answer to your question, than unreliable information from posting on social media groups.

OUTSOURCE

Some tasks are better to outsource if you don't have the skillset, or if you want to be 100% certain you are complying with regulations. We outsource our tax returns, company accounts, VAT and payroll to our Accountants.

In the beginning you'll be the jack of all trades. But, at some point you may be stretched so thin in your business, that you will be the roadblock holding it back. In that case, the only way to grow is to start outsourcing to others.

You could jump straight to hiring an employee if revenues allow it. However, most of the people I know with small businesses use contractors for a few hours per week, or Virtual Assistants.

Virtual Assistants are relatively low-cost resources, usually based in India and Philippines. My friends tend to use them on low-value, repetitive tasks, like collating data, sending sales messages, managing social media inboxes and bookkeeping.

I've listed the website we use for one-off jobs in the simplicity tools download, in the Bonus Content area of Chapter 2.

HIRING A TEAM

I've never hired a full-time employee, so I'll share what we learned from a Tony Robbins' Business Mastery course.

The secret to building an effective team is to ensure you have these 3 identity types:

- Artist/Producer
- Manager/Leader
- Entrepreneur

The Artist loves to create things. They're perhaps not so driven by status and tend not to focus on money.

The Manager likes to streamline systems and operations, or keep a team running effectively. They may also be skilled at both.

The Entrepreneur keeps the big picture in mind, takes risks and focuses on building a profitable business.

Picture these 3 identity types as the legs of a stool—if one leg is missing, then the stool falls down!

Sarah and I have an interesting blend.

I'm a *Manager*. I like researching, analysing, building and streamlining systems. I started programming computers when I was

11 and have a degree in Computer Science. Even the process of writing books is a system for me.

Sarah is the *Artist*. She comes up with so many ideas every day. Some are good, and some are not so good! She brings them to me to evaluate—I ask the "And then what?" question.

In addition, we both have a smaller proportion of *Entrepreneur*. Both our parents started small businesses when we were growing up, which gave us the confidence to set up various small businesses of our own. The knowledge and skills from my MBA, together with my previous career in Marketing and General Management also really helped us.

Niche: Your Target Avatar/Client

Let's talk about the magic of the target avatar—it's like talking with your best friend. You know everything about them—including all their pain and desires. When you write a social media post or email, this is who you're talking to. When people with similar backgrounds to the avatar read your communications, they'll think: "Hey, that person is like me"—and they'll join your tribe.

It's much simpler to target a particular audience, rather than trying to reach everyone on the planet. **Selecting a niche will set you apart from everyone else and usually attract more customers than targeting everyone.**

I'm often on business calls where people don't know which niche and avatar to choose. The rule of thumb that I've successfully followed is twofold:

Option A: Your Old Self

If you've been on a transformational journey to conquer a problem, then that is my favourite choice. You know exactly the pain and desires you started with—now, with the gift of hindsight, you've got the roadmap to a faster transformation.

Your experience is unique. Take our journey, for instance. We quit corporate life and achieved financial freedom by the time Sarah was 39 years old. Or when Sarah shed 56 pounds to hit reach her ideal bodyweight.

Maybe you went from battling an eating disorder to having total control of your food?

Or from infertility to IVF, or adopting a baby?

Or you successfully kicked alcohol addiction to live that sober life?

Everyone's got a story—a journey from pain to transformation. It's a shining beacon for others, letting them know they're not alone.

Option B: Explore Your Passions

There are times when working with people who remind you of your former self can be challenging. It stirs up unpleasant memories and takes a toll on your emotional well-being. In such instances, consider turning to your passions instead. What truly ignites your enthusiasm right now?

For instance, when I started a Personal Training business, I targeted everyone. This wasn't niche enough. Nobody knew why I was the only choice for them. I found it hard to get new clients and attracted people I didn't really want to work with. The problem was that they didn't know what I stood for.

In my personal workouts, I trained for strength by lifting heavy weights and doing calisthenics. That's what I enjoyed. When I changed my communications to focus on that, my business improved. I was THE ONLY calisthenics instructor for at least 20 miles. I was the only Personal Trainer in my town that looked strong. The combination of the two became a strength, not a weakness. The result: my client list started expanding, and I got joy from seeing my clients grow in strength and self-confidence.

What you perceive as your weakness, preventing you from attracting customers, might be your hidden strength.

Perhaps you're a singer who teaches yoga techniques for singers; a gluten intolerant baker who only makes gluten-free cupcakes; or a woman with Parkinson's disease teaching exercise to Parkinson's patients. Embrace not only you're your strengths, but also your weaknesses and weirdness.

Consider the case of Bethany Hamilton. She had one arm bitten off by a 14-foot long tiger shark. Later she became a professional surfer—inspiring amputees to become unstoppable. She's authored books, there's a documentary on her life, and she works with youth and amputees to help them overcome their difficulties, by giving them hope.

Moreover, whether you choose to connect with your past-self, or align with your current passions, remember "And then what?"

Ask yourself: "What will it be like to focus your energies on people that are like your avatar?"

So, create your unique niche, embody that avatar, and let's transform lives!

STRUCTURING YOUR PRODUCT OFFERINGS

Your products and services should fit the needs of your target avatar—leading to the transformation they desire.

However, sometimes what people think they want, might not be what they actually need. Take the classic case of someone wanting a detailed diet plan to shed a few pounds. What they might actually need is a toolkit to tackle stress, and learn the importance of sleep, so they don't turn into a midnight snack bandit.

So, here's the trick—focus mainly on communicating what they want, and subtly include the tools that will help them the most.

Let's talk about specific offerings and pricings. **It's useful to have a product staircase.** This begins with an entry-level product with low pricing, to help customers to get to know you, and the value you provide.

As customers ascend the product staircase, they are offered products with much more value, commanding a higher price. You might also decide to offer coaching or mentoring. Whatever you offer, always keep the customers desired transformation in mind.

The golden rule is to keep the number of product offerings simple—otherwise you'll confuse your clients and make less money.

Here's the proof. A study conducted by Stanford and Columbia Universities, tested the effect of offering shoppers 6, versus 24 different types of jam.[12]

They found a tenfold difference in spend! Thirty percent of people who were only shown 6 jam varieties made a purchase. Conversely, only three percent of those who were shown the more extensive range actually bought. Simplicity wins again!

COMMUNICATION CHANNELS

Navigating the huge and ever-changing social media landscape is like trying to choose the best flavour at an ice cream shop—overwhelming, with a risk of brain freeze if you're not careful!

After juggling many social media platforms, I realised I was spreading myself too thin. My biggest presence was on two channels. The main one was where people my age were hanging out—those were the people I related to the most.

The other channel had the biggest following, but I was inundated by people direct messaging me to sell something—eventually I said farewell and deleted my account.

Each social media channel account you add is like adopting a high-maintenance pet. You need to feed it with posts, groom it with replies, and take it for a walk through the notifications. Instead, consider focusing on just one or two platforms, and go deep.

But there's one exception to this digital socialising—enter the king of communication, email. **Your email list is the VIP access to your audience.** Social media platforms might stop showing your posts, or even go out of business, but your email list? That should be the lifeline of your business.

You don't need many emails to have a successful business. With the right products, and the right high-level offers priced at many thousands of pounds, it's possible to make a 6-figure income from just 1,000 people on your email list. However, they must be true fans of yours, who are highly engaged and understand you. Quality, over quantity.

So, buckle up and start building your email list today! Begin with an opt-in landing page to register for your mailing list and graduate to offering downloadable goodies or access to private areas.

And don't be one of those people who only sends emails to "buy my stuff." Give your audience value with teaching points, freebies, event invites and tell them what you're up to.

3 Ways to Grow Your Business

These are to: Increase your clients, increase the average transaction value and increase frequency of purchase

1. Increase your Clients

Increase the number of people you promote your products and services to. Also increase the frequency that you communicate with your audience on your email list and social media channels.

Spend time increasing your conversion rate. How can you make your opt-in landing pages more effective?

2. Increase the Average Transaction Value

Consider upselling customers to more valuable products at a higher price. You could also introduce bundles which save the customer money and give you more revenue overall.

3. Increase the Frequency of Purchase

Give special offers to encourage customers to book again. Alternatively, provide subscription or membership options.

Next, we'll hear from Sarah Beth, at Sarah Beth Yoga on how she simplified her life, improved her wellbeing, and grew a 7-figure business through delegating.

Interview: Sarah Beth, Sarah Beth Yoga

How did your business start?

When I started this business, I was pretty young. I got my teacher training when I was 21 years old and I was teaching in person at yoga studios a few times a week.

My husband is very entrepreneurial, and we were dating at the time, so he was inspiring me to start building a business online.

I started my YouTube channel back in 2010. I was a chiropractic assistant in 2012, and by 2013 I'd quit that to start doing YouTube full time. Because I was so excited about what I was doing, I was working all the time. We were both young and didn't have a lot else going on, so it felt good to be building something.

Who cares if we go to bed at 3 in the morning?

Who cares if we sleep in?

Who cares if we have dinner a little late?

But over time, you start to recognize how it's negatively affecting your life, and you don't really know how to adjust things. Also, there was no push or urgency to change things, because we were in our twenties and no one else was dependent on me.

There's like an over worker, high achiever within me, that will still want to work till 3 am. But I have boundaries at this point in my life. It's in me, and I get it when I see it in other people. Cause I'm like, yeah, I did that! And it was fun—and they like it, because there's a piece of you that wants to do it, and it feels good.

Even though it's a sacrifice—you're willing to sacrifice a good night's sleep because you know that you're building something, and you're so enthusiastic about it.

When did you realise you were pushing yourself too hard?

At the time, I was starting to realise it wasn't sustainable, and it wasn't healthy. How do I continue building a business without doing it this way?

So, I asked a friend of mine who was also doing something similar to me, how she was creating boundaries in her life, and why she had structure and I didn't. She said it was because she had kids. Things just have to change, and structure naturally falls into place.

I did a lot of inner work for my mental health the year prior to having my baby. It was addressing a disconnection between how I was living my life and who I truly was. There was a misalignment there.

When I gave birth and with all of the changes in hormones, I didn't realise the mental health issues that needed addressing. If you ignore it, it's only going to continue to get worse—and that was kind of what was happening with me.

I was in this hustle culture. I was living in my business and I liked it. I had this nesting energy: I want to do this; I want to build this; I love my community; I love what I'm making. But now, I need to sleep, take care of myself, and take care of someone else. And on top of all of that, I had postpartum depression and anxiety, which I also didn't recognise. I'm so good at convincing myself that "I'm fine."

When my son was 3 months old, we went to a family reunion. We were with 40 family members standing on a deck off the back of a house, about to take a photo. So, the guy taking the photo is standing on the ground far away. He said, 3, 2…and as he's about to click the shutter, the deck collapses!

The part attached to the house was still attached, and the outside part fell down. So, everyone slid down. I was holding my baby and behind me was his great grandfather who was 89. So, I'm thinking youngest, oldest and is everyone okay?

Luckily, no one died. But there were broken backs and at least a dozen members in the hospital for multiple nights.

It was a very traumatic event. A lot of us walked away with PTSD, but we didn't know how to deal with something like that. Most of us couldn't get on an elevator for months after that, afraid of falling again.

My baby was fine. I ended up bringing him to the hospital and he got checked over. He just had some scratches on him. I had a large hematoma on my hip—now it's just scar tissue. I also sprained my ankle.

That event was the catalyst for me to finally see a therapist. Because now I had some real PTSD symptoms—I didn't even want to stand on a third-floor apartment building. I didn't want to be in a group with too many people in a room.

Because I had this sense of urgency, I booked the first therapist I called that was available. I would have picked a female therapist, but this man answers and I'm like, "Yep, I'm coming in right now if you're available." I ended up working with him for 5 years, and he was such a good fit for me.

We worked through the PTSD stuff really quickly. What was actually underlying all of that was postpartum anxiety and postpartum depression. And what was underlying that, was a lifetime of mental health issues that had never been addressed. And what was underlying that, was childhood trauma.

How did you create balance in your life?

It was then that I actually started to create more balance in my life. The new balance I started to see in my personal life was reflecting in my professional work. I created boundaries and containment. I contained my work to a space or a desk, and I didn't take that work over into my bed or the living room. I didn't take that work with me when I was playing with my son. That containment was my first step towards creating more of that balance. The more that I felt better aligned and having more self-compassion, the more I was able to better serve my community.

But there was still this deep guilt that I wasn't doing enough, because I'd set a high bar. I was uploading videos as frequently as possible, and to create balance, I had to pull away from that frequency. So, I reduced the quantity of my video uploads and posts. But the people who stuck around started to see the quality increase.

Looking back, I think I still had lingering burnout for several years. While I was doing the inner work, the personal work, and navigating mental health, I started to notice: this is what anxiety feels like; this is what depression feels like; this is how I find more balance in my life.

To get that pendulum swinging from anxiety to depression, you maybe need to slow down and start to find a little bit of this inner space. But also, being okay with the fact that I might get triggered and thrown into one side, or the other. Finding acceptance is the hardest part. Everything I'm talking about, is everything that I've been teaching.

The cone of learning shows that if somebody is reading something, they only retain 10% of it. If they hear it, they retain 20%. If they see it, it's 30%—it's all passive.

But say it and write it down, and you start to retain up to 70% of it. When you start to do it. It's 90%. And then there's even more when you teach it. I practice a lot of that kind of learning in my life. Once I learn it, I teach it. And I always teach based off my personal experience. So that's why I don't teach headstands and handstands. It helps me to be an authentic teacher. People feel like I'm really truly talking to them, because I'm teaching from a place of experience.

What I've loved so much about yoga is that everything I've been doing in terms of personal development is like a branch of yoga. It is self-observation; It is acceptance; It is mindfulness.

How did you delegate to simplify your life?

As I reflect back to those years of me learning to balance my life, I can see there was still so much burnout to navigate. I was starting to ask people, "How do I do this?"

There was no manual back in 2012 for running a business as a solo entrepreneur. So, then I started reaching out and looking for it. I was listening to podcasts and looking for anyone I could find that was like me.

I ended up going to a John Demartini seminar, where he spoke about identifying your highest values and living in line with them. Afterwards, I asked him, "Hey, my son was born recently, and I'm dealing with a lot. I used to be able to manage things and I built this amazing business, and I want to continue building it, but I also really want to focus on my son. I always wanted to be a mother, but I'm really struggling doing both."

He told me to figure out what my 3 highest values were, and then delegate the rest. At the time they were security, family and growth. Now it's actually security, connection and growth—because I found that family falls within the connection piece. But I'm really thriving on connecting with other people now.

At the time I was making close to $1,200 a month in advertising revenue off YouTube, which was pretty good. I saw that if I uploaded a little more...I made a little more. But it wasn't enough money to bring in full time help. So, I was having a really hard time with that.

When I was pregnant with my son, I went and got a prenatal certification to teach yoga. Then I created a prenatal program while I was pregnant, because I knew what a pregnant body would feel like in those poses. By the time my son was born, we had launched the prenatal yoga program as a digital product for sale. Before that, I only had AdSense revenue. I also started launching a couple of one-off sales.

About a year after I gave birth to my son, my income increased to $4,000 a month of passive revenue. And that was the point when I started to delegate. I began with hiring a mother's helper—a young girl who would come over and just play with my son while I was working. I tried hiring a house cleaner once a month, but it was really hard for me because I had these limiting beliefs—"Why pay someone to do something that I could do myself."

Because of the state of my mental health at the time, I was isolating myself and didn't have much of a network. I wasn't around people who might know how to do what I'm doing. So, in my own bubble, only I knew about running my business. No one could help.

I used to model when I was younger, so I have friends that are photographers and know about lighting. So, every once in while I'd ask for their help. But asking beyond that, caused me to come up against my limiting belief, that I would not be able to find people to help.

I slowly started working through the limiting belief, by first hiring consultants for SEO and automating things to make my life a little easier.

I got to a point in 2019 when I was able to hire my first employee—Paige. It was a scary commitment for me at the time, but she's still with me and I'm so grateful—she was such a great choice for me. I had heard through the grapevine that she was looking for a job. I was asked by a CEO of another company, whether I would recommend her. And I said, "You would be a fool not to hire her. She is so respectful and tactful, and she figures everything out. She will handle problems and she communicates so well." I tried to explain all of this to the CEO and they were like, "yeah, you know, I'm not sure."

At that time, I was at a Tony Robbins' mastery seminar, and they were talking about how every business needs three identities in their business. You need an artist, entrepreneur and a manager—like the three legs of a stool. That's when I realised that one of the issues we were having, is my husband was the entrepreneur and I was the artist. But we didn't have a manager. That was a light bulb moment for me. I thought "I've got to hire Paige," she's gonna be the third leg of that stool.

It was a monumental step for me in my business and in my personal life, because I was able to delegate. I could trust her to take so much off of my plate.

Another limiting belief that I had before I hired her, was that in order for a woman to be taken seriously, I had to be a mean boss. I thought I needed to be very rigid, very stern, and very serious. I thought I needed to be like the character Miranda Priestly in The Devil Wears Prada.

I worked through that by reframing and telling myself, that I could be like Sara Blakely—the founder of Spanx. She is fun, lovely and very light-hearted. You feel like you're friends with her, and she runs this amazing company, doing amazing things. She's got a family, so I decided to run my business like I'm Sara Blakely.

I started that with Paige. She got me to a place where I had more capacity in my life—because now she was taking care of all the emails, and I trusted her to take care of the customers. I could hand off problems to her and say, "I don't know how to do this. Can you figure this out?" She'd tell me, "I've got it. I'll figure this out."

I was figuring out what hats I was wearing in my business. I already knew she'd wear the customer service hat and the product management hat. It brought me so much relief—it was a sigh, instead of a gasp.

My next hire for production, filming and editing was a lot harder, because I already had a vision. I had been doing this for years. So, when I brought other people in, they didn't know my vision as well as I did. They were quoting huge prices. And I'd say, "No, we don't need a huge set and eight grips. No, we just need this one wall and enough lighting to fill it. And we need just one camera, with one person to sit on the camera and make sure that it doesn't overheat. Then I need one person to edit this and I'll show you exactly how to edit."

I definitely had some challenges with it. There were misunderstandings of how much work was going to be required—

because traditionally it is something that's being filmed in a production studio. They're working way harder, like on Budweiser commercials and Lamborghini commercials.

I'm like, "I'm just gonna put my mat right here. We're gonna do the one shot. That's it." I'm all about working smarter, not harder. So, production definitely came with growing pains. But what was nice was that I persisted. And every time that we ran into an issue, I learned to create an "if then" statement. If this happens, then do this—then you just give it to your whole team. So, we just learned and got better, and better and better. When the studio shut down, we had to find a new studio space. When that opportunity ended, the next opportunity was even better. We would never have found that studio if it hadn't ended.

So, fast forward a couple of years and I'm speaking at VidSummit in 2019, which is a video marketing conference. I was doing a speech about how to scale your business. At the time I had an employee, a team of contractors, my business was doing 6 figures, and I had around 800,000 subscribers on YouTube.

I was doing this speech, and I didn't realise that it was going to open up a lot more opportunities, through just connection. This was a turning point for me in my isolation. It showed me that by being present and by connecting with people, which I actually really do enjoy, it creates opportunities. I ended up meeting Jason, who is now my lead videographer and editor, and he's on my leadership team. I met him—he was a friendly guy, and tall like my husband. So, I asked my husband to go and talk to him, and they became friends. Over several months, I watched them work together. Then there was a point where my editor wanted to move on into a different role, and I'm looking for a new editor. My husband asks, "What about Jason?" Jason has a background with yoga and wellness, and he's a rock climber. So, we brought Jason in, and it ended up being a fit that just got better and better, the more we worked together.

Then just two years ago we started on Entrepreneurial Operating System (EOS). It is like a manual for small business. It comes with a coach and you bring the whole team together, to do day long sessions of working on the business, not in the business. The promise from that coach was that we would relieve my stress, because I was still operating from a place of overwhelm. Even though I had delegated, I just kept filling in those gaps.

I felt like my norm for work was way up here, and that if I'm delegating and start doing less, that people around me would think, "Oh, she's just getting me to work so she can kick her feet up." I was afraid people would call me lazy. That was my limiting belief. Versus maybe this is an opportunity for me to not work a 120-hour work week. But, by adopting this operating system and bringing my entire team together to create a vision, brand values, mission, goals and weekly meetings—it started to show that I was able to take my foot off the gas.

I look forward to my weekly meetings, because I'm delegating, and I know that the work is going to get done. My team is excited to work on these things. At the same time, I'm warning them to take care of themselves. It's very important that when you wake up in the morning, you don't just immediately open up your email. Take your time. If you want to go work out in the middle of the day, then go work out. Do you want to go on vacation? One of our team values is, "GSD and Chill"—get shit done and chill. So yeah, you can go on vacation, just get your shit done first. I'm not expecting things at specific hours, Monday through Friday.

How has your business and home life changed since you hired a team?

The business is running over seven figures consistently. I have a team of four on my leadership team, and we have several contractors underneath each of our team members.

Those numbers are exciting and impressive—but the most exciting piece for me is that I feel grounded. I launched my book *Trauma Alchemy* back in April, and that was the last time where I felt like I was burning out again, because the book launch was so much. And basically, since September, I've been living from a parasympathetic nervous system. I've always been vulnerable in my authenticity, but

I'm now more vulnerable with the people that I'm leading. My leadership team are like my support system. And I'll just say to them, "Hey, it might not look like I'm working much this week, but I'm gonna be taking care of myself and still working on things." Sometimes I'll get verbal confirmation like "We don't think you're lazy. Don't worry if you want to kick up your feet."

There were years where my yoga practice was purely to create for others. I fell out of love with it for my personal practice. I never thought I was ever going to get it back. But, I'm now at a place where I've reconnected with my yoga practice. Introducing psychedelics as medicine over the last two years, has been a huge piece of my mental health.

Everything is amazing in my business. More is not more at this point. I still have consultants telling me essentially that more is more. If you upload more, you make more money. I'm like, more is not more. Less is more right now. I'd rather show up with quality than quantity.

I've been attending retreats personally as a guest—which I haven't done in a very long time. I've also been taking yoga classes, and I've been doing my own personal practice. That is just for me and not for anything else. I'm not sequencing, I'm meditating. The life I'm living right now feels so good and grounded. And I feel like I'm not hungry for more. Life is good. My family is comfortable. My employees are well fed. We don't need to burn ourselves out. So that's where I am now.

What is your daily work and nurturing routine?

I wake up at 5 in the morning. I just take my time as I get dressed, brush my teeth and do my skin care and all that. I don't check anything. I'm not taking any input during that time. Within about 10 minutes of waking up I'll meditate. I do one or two meditations depending on the day—between 10 to 30 minutes of meditation.

After meditation I'll sit there and reflect—maybe journal and think about my day. By 6 o'clock I start heading downstairs to make breakfast for my boys. Now that I'm in this place of capacity, I can be the archetypal mother for my boys. Because when I was at low capacity and low mood, I really struggled with being able to give in the way that I wanted.

So, I make my boys breakfast and I make myself cacao. I stopped drinking coffee a couple months ago and I drink cacao in the morning instead—it's wonderful. A couple days a week I micro dose with psilocybin in my cacao. Then I spend the morning with my boys, talking to them while they're eating their breakfast, and I'm making myself breakfast. It's nice and slow and relaxed. I've got binaural beats playing on our Echo.

So, every day turns out the same and creates this relaxed mood in the house. The mood will pick up a little bit when it's like, "All right, brush and floss. Let's leave for school." But once they're out the door and they leave for school, I've got about 45 minutes with the house to myself, because my husband takes them to school in the morning.

During that time from 7.15 to 8 o'clock, I follow this PRE-WORK RITUAL.

[She pulls out a card]

1. SET the SETTING

- I turn on the heat in my office.

- I turn on music in my headphones.

- I use Palo Santo to create a setting in my office.

2. MOVE

- After that I'll move my body. I close my eyes and just move in a dancing, kind of therapeutic, somatic way—just to one song. I look at the dancing as completing the stress cycle. So, if I've had some stress, I'm gonna start shaking it out. Or, sometimes it turns into yoga.

- Move Pain Free Recode program: I'm doing this functional movement program. You get this personalized recode for your body, with a series of functional movement exercises, to help address specific alignment issues within your own body. You send in a video of you standing in four different poses, then you walk away…then run away and run back. They watch it and then tell you things like, "Okay your right hip is doing this, and it's causing your ankle to do this, and if you don't fix that over time it's gonna cause this issue." Then they give you the exercises specific to your body.

3. MEDITATE

- Then I do a silent five-minute meditation. It's a little reset moment.

- Sometimes I add in a singing bowl, because I love sound therapy.

4. MINDSET

- Then I just sit down at my desk and review my tasks for the day.

* * * * *

My husband gets home at 8 o'clock, and for the next hour we've adopted this thing that we call the "Love Hour." The reason that we started doing this, is because we went to couples counselling a few years ago, because we both work from home. We work in the same business together, run this house, these kids and everything together. It's a lot, you know. We spend so much time with each other, that going on a regular date night isn't hitting it like it used to. Back then, couple's counselling really helped us learn how to navigate this new territory, and communicate with each other. I suggested that we do couples counselling again last fall, because I could tell that there was some dysfunction within how we were carrying ourselves and communicating with each other. There were new responsibilities on the table, and he suggested that we do the Tony Robbins Ultimate Relationship Program first. We needed to do it every day if were gonna prioritise it. We worked on this program together. It's only supposed to last 10 days, but some questions would spark a conversation that lasted the entire hour. So, we spent three months on it—just taking our sweet time. But it was so good for us. Now that we're getting to the end of the Tony Robbins program, we're like, "Okay, how can we use the Love Hour to continue to connect with each other?"

Now we're learning to dance in our Love Hour. We're using this online dance lesson program called "Show Her Off." It's written for the male of the dance partner couple. It's similar to swing, I think. It's spinney and twirly. It's really fun. We find that we're able to progress really quickly. After we learned three moves, we could dance a whole song.

Nine o'clock is when I finally will sit down at my computer, and open up my email and Slack. I already know what my tasks are for the day, because I did that during my pre-work ritual. I'm mentally prepared for my first big task, and I'm gonna start working on that.

At noon I allow myself to have lunch without screens. What I really like doing is reading while I'm eating. I take my time to eat my lunch, and after that I'll lay down on my acupressure mat for non-sleep deep rest—Yoga Nidra. I do that for 20 to 30 minutes. It's so rejuvenating.

At 1 o'clock, I'll either, have a meeting, run an errand, or finish up a little bit of work.

By 2 o'clock, I have my post work ritual, which is the opposite side of this.

[She flips the card over]

POST WORK RITUAL

It's the same thing as the pre-work ritual, but in a different order.

1. MINDSET.

- Finish the task I was working on, or email.

- Then I start to set tomorrow's tasks. So, everything is written down—and by doing that, I'm mentally telling myself that I'm done with this until tomorrow. Which is really important for me, because otherwise I just feel like I need to continue working.

2. SET THE SETTING

- I tidy up my space.

- I'll do the Palo Santo again.

- I'll turn on music.

3. MOVE

Again, it's just one song, where I might dance or do yoga. I'm thinking about whatever I need to do, to clear the stress cycle.

4. MEDITATE

- Then I do a 5-minute meditation.

* * * * *

By 3 o'clock, I'm done for the day. I leave to go pick up my boys from school, and I'm not thinking about work. I'm ready to talk to them about their day, and how they feel. I'm actually listening to them, and interested in what they're saying.

When they get home, I get them going on their responsibilities, and I'll start thinking about dinner. I cook three times a week, and my husband cooks three times a week. We do take out one night a week. We eat dinner pretty early at 5.30 pm, then it's this whole, long bedtime routine. If the boys can get their bedtime routine done sooner, then they can play on screens for a little bit.

When they're getting ready for bed at seven o'clock, I'm getting ready for bed. When they're brushing their teeth, I'm brushing my teeth. I'm putting on PJs. I'm so excited because it's just feels good. By the time they're in bed and we give good night kisses, I am ready to be in my bed.

First, I'll journal. I'm actually doing a lot more process journaling, to process out something that I need to think about. I'll ask myself questions and answer them.

My lights are out by 8.30 pm and I am asleep, happily knowing that I'm gonna wake up again at 5 o'clock the next day, and do it again.

Before I had kids, when I was working 120 hours a week—I would wake up whenever I wanted to, and probably sleep until 10 in the morning. I would immediately open up my phone and email, which I don't even keep on my phone anymore—I don't have any social media on my phone either. I have huge boundaries there. And while I was working, laptop in hand, I'd go grab some food and eat it. I'd keep working and eating my food. I probably didn't even get out of my PJs. It was just kind of like that throughout the entire day. At some point we'd have dinner and watch a show together, then I'd be excited to get more work done.

That was a time in my life. That was a phase. I'm not dogging it, because it was the high achiever part of me that got me to where I am. But I could have learned to refine it so much sooner. I think it would have helped me to find my balance in my wellness.

I have friends here right now, who are working that very long day lifestyle. They're building their businesses online, and I can see the enthusiasm and excitement that they have for it. They're asking me about my lifestyle, because it is just so different from theirs. I explain to them that if I really had a big project, the most amount of time that I have in a day to work on it is 5 hours. That's between 9 am and 2 pm—and even then, a girl's got to have lunch. I'm not going to work and eat lunch at the same time. So, I don't tend to be able to get full projects done in one sitting, the way that the overachiever in me wants to. I have to practice being okay with that. But it's a worthy trade off. The project's still gonna get done, but I feel better. And something I have to remind myself, is that there's always going to be more work to do.

FOLLOW SARAH BETH:

Website: sarahbethyoga.com
SarahBethYoga App bit.ly/SBYAPP

YouTube: @sarahbethyoga
Instagram: @sarahbethyoga
Facebook: @SarahBethYoga

Author of:
Trauma Alchemy: Transform Hardship, Stress, and Trauma into Your Best Life through Yoga

Conclusion: Work and Mission

This chapter has been a rollercoaster through the productivity landscape—getting stuff done, toppling big domino goals, giving the boot to busywork, and embracing imperfection.

You've learned the art of saying no to endless meetings, discovered the magic of focusing during high-productivity hours, and mastered the inbox monster.

You've learned the simple ways to grow your business and income.

We've asked the crucial questions: Are you in the right job? And are you getting paid even less than you think?

With inspiration from Sarah Beth, of Sarah Beth Yoga, we've witnessed the transformative power of delegation for simplifying life and growing your business.

So, buckle up, as we move onto nurturing and simplifying your relationships.

CHAPTER 7

Nurturing Healthy Relationships

"Where there is love there is life."
— *Mahatma Gandhi*

In this chapter, we embark on a journey to discover the transformative power of simplifying relationships, to create a harmonious symphony in our lives.

As we delve into the art of simplification, we find that it is not about diminishing the significance of our relationships, but rather about surrounding ourselves with greatness.

From shedding toxic relationships, to adopting effective communication strategies, we navigate the path to relationship simplicity.

We'll draw inspiration from the experiences of International Opera Singer, Deanna Breiwick, who reveals her personal journey of simplifying relationships, to forge the strongest support system of her life.

Through Deanna's insights, we gain a glimpse into the transformative power of making intentional connections and the profound impact they can have on our well-being.

As you assess your Relationships, keep in mind the Simplicity Secret Tool:

D — Delete
O — Outsource
S — Substitute
H — Habitulise

↓

AND THEN WHAT?

SIMPLICITY SECRET

Close relationships are the cornerstone of my existence, providing support in challenging times and celebrating my wins. These people serve as a sanctuary for sharing my private questions, hopes and dreams—**they're essential for my emotional well-being.** They're the force that guides me forward, preventing me from crumbling in hard times.

The dynamics of personal and professional relationships can either propel you to your destiny, or send you into a downward spiral with catastrophic results.

Sarah and I spend time on continual and never-ending improvement (CANI) in our marriage and business life. Just as the artificial intelligence machine in the movie Oblivion queried, "Are you still an effective team…?"—we ask ourselves the same question…but without the killer robots!

Now, that doesn't mean Sarah and I have a perfect relationship. Far from it. Often, kids, work, and other things can take priority, and before you know it, you realise you haven't been out on a date for a month! **But what we do have is open and honest chats with each**

other every day, to address things that are not going well, or are being neglected. We don't agree on everything, but openness, acceptance and occasional conceding helps. We're committed to maintaining and improving our relationship, as it's the glue that holds our family and business life together.

But what about other people?

Navigating the complexities of relationships requires accepting that people are imperfect, and you can't change them—they need to do that for themselves. **Occasionally it's time to delete negative people from your contacts list.**

Join the simplicity movement. Simplifying your relationships is key to fostering meaningful connections and attaining harmony in your life.

SURROUND YOURSELF WITH GREATNESS

> *"You are the average of the five people you spend the most time with.*
> *— Jim Rohn*

When I first read that quote, I took a long hard look at my friends list. Most of them weren't going where I wanted to go. I wanted to invest in property to become financially free. None of them fitted that criteria, or believed it was possible.

When you aim higher, the quality of your conversations with friends completely changes. Instead of them talking about how "money doesn't grow on trees" and despising wealthy people, the conversations are focused on where to invest, how to save tax and how to ensure a legacy for your loved ones.

Or, perhaps you'd like an outlet for talking about spirituality and manifesting, but your current friends would just ridicule you for mentioning woo-woo topics like that?

SIMPLICITY SECRET

When you make new friends who are into spirituality, conversations are all about meditation, healing, enlightenment, bliss and eliminating suffering.

Show me your friends and I'll show you your future. Take a good look at the five people you talk with the most each week and ask yourself:

Do you desire their life?

Or do you aspire to something greater?

> *Proximity is power!*
> *If you want to have an extraordinary life surround yourself with people who make you better.*
> *—Tony Robbins*

If you want more from your friendships, substitute some of your current friends with people that have qualities you admire. You don't need to confront your old friends and hit the ejector seat—you can just let the relationship fizzle out over time.

If you plan to befriend people at a much higher level, let's not forget the rule of fair exchange. These people may not hang around in your circles, unless you can provide them with value in return. If you've got skills they desire, then that's great. But I'm not adverse to buying my way in—sometimes the only way to get a seat at the table is to pay them to mentor you for a year, or to join their membership.

I used to have a long list of friends—but when you have that many you don't have the opportunity to build deep and meaningful relationships. **Now, I have just three small groups of friends representing most of my interests.**

If you enter a new friendship group, be your authentic self and share your vulnerability.

LETTING GO OF TOXIC RELATIONSHIPS

You might be so used to having energy vampires sucking the blood out of your life, that you've never considered how your mental health would improve by letting go of them.

You need to recognise the signs. Is there anyone in your life who continually does things that make you feel frustrated, angry or resentful? Perhaps you can't be your authentic self with them, for fear of being ridiculed, or just not understood.

Personally, I refuse to work or spend time with people who act unethically, or who are constantly negative.

I've been there. I had a close friend that was like a ticking time bomb, waiting to explode in anger at any moment. I was constantly walking around on eggshells. Her life was like a reality show, always seeking attention—late entrances, squeezing sympathy out of others, and turning mundane events into blockbuster dramas. After enduring this for many years, one day I reached my breaking point. She made a comment that felt like a punch to the gut, at a time my emotions were so fragile. **That was the moment I realised I didn't need to have the constant drama and negativity occupying my life**. I could choose a different path. I swiftly left and cut my ties from that day. It was a messy break up, but it's a relief not to be caught in the whirlwind of drama anymore.

COMMUNICATION STRATEGIES FOR RELATIONSHIP SIMPLICITY

If you've seen me on a video, or presenting at a conference, you'd probably never guess that I'm an introvert. I prefer small groups and can get tired out by large crowds. I'm like a solitary cat at network meetings. I just want to find a quiet corner to sit in, as I feel awkward striking up conversations with strangers. On the other hand, Sarah is a social butterfly—she's my anchor when we go to a party or other event. I just follow her around.

In the past, I'd never been great at keeping in touch with friends. Looking back to when I was a child, I tended to have only one BFF who I'd spend night and day with, and then a lot of friends on the fringe who I never got to know that well. Over the years I've lost touch with most of my BFF's, feeling embarrassed to call them up after so long.

More recently, I've found it best to *habitualise* my friendship garden, so that I can ensure I keep watering the flowers and bring them into full bloom. I currently have three small groups of friends, whom I intentionally sought out to fulfil different passions and interests of mine. We have regular weekly or monthly social get togethers, usually over Zoom. Scheduling regular calls helps avoid reaching that awkward point where it's been so long that I'm too embarrassed to contact them.

I even schedule in my family. Although Sarah and I often spend 24 hours a day with each other, we are generally doing our own thing. For example, I'm writing this book right now while she's reading a book, doing a course, or practicing her choir songs.

To compensate, Sarah and I have a recurring appointment in our diary to have "chat time" every afternoon. We make a cup of tea and sit somewhere quiet, with no distractions. We discuss how to improve all parts of our life, or anything on our mind. This is also time for me to be open with my emotions, which was difficult for me in the past, as I tended to keep them hidden. We often talk about something we've read in a book that could be useful to us. We talk about openly everything: money, relationship, sex, kids, spirituality, anything really. Occasionally we'll read a relationship book, or re-watch Tony Robbins Ultimate Relationship Program and work through that. We also have one "Date Day" a week, when our kids go to their grandparents.

In addition, we have one-to-one chat time with our two teenage children at bedtime. We spend half an hour separately with each of them, doing whatever they want—but not playing computer games. It's our opportunity to fully connect with them. Yesterday I was colouring in a mosaic fish with my daughter. Other times we play charades or monopoly. Occasionally we play hide and seek, or physical games, which is still fun for a teenager (and us)!

Moreover, I have a scheduled video call or in-person lunch with my mother every week, and we see Sarah's family multiple times per week as they live close by.

Balancing Personal and Professional Connections

Navigating the tightrope of personal and professional connections is like juggling flaming torches—enthralling, but with a hint of danger.

For instance, we have a good friend who became one of our paid mentees. We had to maintain a strict separation between social chats and our mentoring sessions.

As time passed, many of our students graduated from mentees to good friends. Nowadays we mostly aim to keep the conversation on social topics and only occasionally discussing "work".

So, if you have people in your life that sit on the edge of personal and professional, consider setting boundaries to ensure there is fair exchange and balance in the relationships.

Interview: Deanna Breiwick, International Opera Singer & Voice Coach

What is your busy travel schedule like as an opera singer?

It depends. Sometimes I've been on the road eleven out of twelve months. So, there's been some years where I'm just literally on the road constantly. I'm home for two days…then I'm unpacking, repacking and getting back out to catch a flight. Then there's other times where I'll have a gig, and then I have a couple of months off.

One of the fun parts about travelling is that sometimes I'm in the vicinity of one of my friends, so we make a plan to get together—and that's always really fun.

Why are your friendships so important to you?

I think with my schedule, there's a lot of groundlessness—I'm always in motion. So over time, my friendships have become my anchors. I have some friends on the ground here in Seattle, but my closest friends are all long-distance friendships. I make more intentional effort to maintain my friendships, because I'm so far away from them. I've got these different types of friendships that sustain me in various parts of my life.

How have negative relationships complicated your life in the past?

There was a time when my group of friends was much larger. However, I found that I had to censor myself around some friends and be careful about what I shared. So, if I was having success…if good things were happening, I didn't want to share out of fear of them being jealous and finding ways to bring me down—maybe not directly in that moment, but in other ways.

Let's say it was another singer that was jealous of some career success. They wouldn't mention that, they'd come after some other part of me like my intelligence, or something else. Friends were looking for ways to set themselves above me in other parts of my life. At first, I just brushed it off—but after a while I thought to myself "no", this really wasn't kind. It wasn't supportive. I was finding more and more that I wasn't able to be myself with them.

How have you simplified and transformed your friendships?

I've reduced the number of friends to a core group. Now I have friends who I can 100% be myself around them. I can share exactly what's going on—the good and the bad. I don't have to censor myself. I don't have to curate how I'm sharing myself with them. I feel safe with them.

I think a lot of that has also come from learning how to support myself better. Becoming my own best friend, cheerleader and support system. And once I started feeling stronger from within, I was less apt to tolerate negativity from some of my previous friends. Some of my friends I've had around for almost a lifetime—and they've also gone through their own evolutions and seasons. But I have this inner circle of friends now that are 100% with me, and I'm 100% with them. It is one of the strongest support systems in my life.

Was there a pivotal moment when you'd decided it was time to change your relationships?

I don't think there was one dramatic point. But I recall an instance when I was in a romantic relationship. Last summer I was taking a leadership and voice course with Happy Jack. There were sections on defining your mission statement and your dream life. There was also a lot about self-leadership, which was a concept that in many ways I was practicing but had never identified. I saw things so crystal clear in that moment—we were not looking at life the same way. And the reality is, there's a lot of people out there who were not going to see life the same way. That's life and humanity.

And as the core circle of friends that I'd been building was becoming stronger, I realised how much support I was drawing from them—it was like a renewable source of energy running between us. And I remember thinking in that moment—I have more of that with my friends than I do with this boyfriend that I'd been dating for a long time. I had more of this synergy and life-giving energy exchange—we were on the same wavelength. So that was a big moment for me when I realised that I had this with my friends, but not with my boyfriend.

With the negative friends, I just stopped putting as much energy and intention into building the connection there. I let the relationships fizzle out. However, one of them is interesting—I had a friend who often came out with comments to put me down. I remember I got to the point where I needed to either talk to her and tell her how it made me feel, or I needed the relationship to end. The relationship was starting to really hurt me. Instead, I mostly gave it a little time, because I knew the kind of upbringing she had, and I realized that some of this might be normal to her—which gave me more compassion. It doesn't excuse the behaviour, but I was able to give it more patience. One time I said to her "Hey, it doesn't feel good when you say that." In a matter of months, she ended up dropping comments like that, and she doesn't do it anymore. She ended up evolving and became part of my inner circle.

As you travel to a lot of cities for your work, how do you choose what to do for fun when there are so many choices?

I always find a coffee shop. I'll try a few over the first few days—then I pick my favourite one and end up going there very regularly. A lot of times when I have a really busy rehearsal schedule, I'm not getting out that much to do fun things. But I will say that when I do have days off, a lot of the fun stuff revolves around food—like finding good restaurants or local specialties. When I was in Dallas earlier, I was Googling for the best for Mexican restaurants, and asking for recommendations. When I was living in Switzerland, or visiting Switzerland, I was searching for the best fondue places. So, I would say, a lot of my favourite things are to do with food.

I also like getting out to natural or green spaces. Some cities have more of a city forest, or maybe a park. On my last trip, I ended up finding this amazing yoga studio, where they also did Reiki and breathwork. I ended up going there really regularly and meeting a lot of cool people. So, I'm pretty low key—I like nature, wellness, food and coffee. And you actually get so much information about the culture of the people there when you do this.

Home Life—as you spend so little time at home, did you decide to simplify your possessions?

I would say, probably compared to most, I'm pretty pared down. I've learned that I don't need that much. For many years I really lived on the road out of my suitcase, which forced me to be a minimalist. In a way, it was it was a really good thing, because it made me think:

Do I really need that sweater?

Do I need that pair of shoes?

Especially for a woman, I probably have a pathetic number of shoes. Although I do have a lot of gowns because of my profession. And I have way too many books—I love reading, so books are the one thing I have not been able to control myself with. But yeah, I would say, it's caused me to simplify.

Every Spring or fall I usually get rid of a lot of stuff. Either I give it away or donate it to charity. This process has also helped me to buy less because when I look at buying something, I think: okay, am I going to get rid of that next year?

Is it going to have lasting value in my life?

And so, I've gotten much choosier. I've also learned about how little I really need—which is mostly just the basics. Also, I find I end up kind of wearing the same outfit every day, because it's comfortable, functional and it makes me happy. Sometimes I'll pack too many clothes and I end up just choosing to wear the same uniform.

When I do purchase things, I really consider their purpose in my life and their usability. So, if it's a piece of clothing—how many different seasons can I wear this in?

How many different kinds of events can I wear this to?

Can I dress it down? And can I dress it up?

Is it comfortable?

How do I feel when I wear it?

Because more and more I've found that if it doesn't feel good, I'm not going to wear it—it's just going to end up sitting there, and I'll give it away. Maybe it seems like a long, or even neurotic process, but it saves me a lot of time later, when I have to find a way to move it out of my life, because I'm not using it.

I was on the road constantly for about four or five years, then the pandemic lockdown happened, so I moved back to my parents' home and put my things into a storage unit. When I started performing in venues again, I was gone the entire year. So, staying at my parents is just a kind of a home base—I have a little room and also my storage unit. Yeah, and that's another thing—I ask myself: if I buy this, am I actually going to use it? Or is it going to go sit in my storage unit?

One funny thing I've been doing is "shopping" in my storage unit. So, if I'm feeling the itch to have something new, I often go to my storage unit first. And oftentimes, if you haven't really seen it or worn it for some months, it feels like a new treasure.

FOLLOW DEANNA BREIWICK:
Instagram: @deannabreiwick
deannabreiwick.com

CONCLUSION: RELATIONSHIPS

Relationships are the melody of life, filling it with purpose, love, and joy—the very air you breathe. Picture your loved ones as vibrant flowers in your emotional garden, demanding continuous care, watering, and occasional weeding out!

Remember that you can't make someone happy—only they hold the power to cultivate their own happiness.

Embrace simplicity, chose your friends wisely, and curate and habitualise your friendship circles.

CHAPTER 8

From Chaos to Calm: Bring Simplicity and Order to Your Home

"Love begins at home, and it is not how much we do... but how much love we put in that action."
—Mother Teresa

Alright, buckle up because we're about to talk about the dark side of a cluttered home—and let me tell you, it has severe effects on your health.

If your living room looks like a wild stag party, then fear not, because in the course of this chapter, we're simplifying the steps to decluttering your house to zen-like serenity.

We'll discuss downsizing and how few material possessions you really need.

There's also an interview with Jack Boken from Happy Jack Yoga, on how simplifying his possessions to follow his passions felt so liberating.

Let's inject some rocket fuel into your home transformation with the Simplicity Secret Tool:

SIMPLICITY SECRET

D Delete **O** Outsource **S** Substitute **H** Habitulise

AND THEN WHAT?

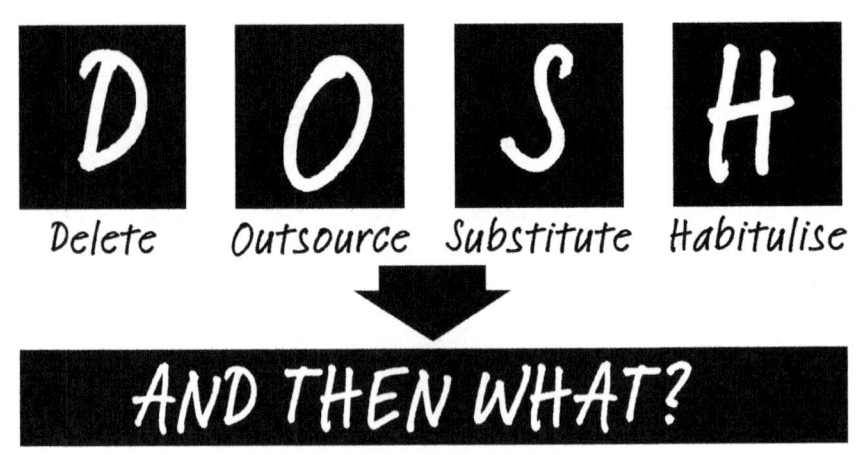

SIMPLICITY SECRET

It's not just a tool; it's a magic wand for decluttering your life. So, ask yourself, will you summon the power to *delete* unnecessary possessions, *outsource* tasks that drain your energy, or *substitute* dissatisfying elements of your home with joy? Better yet, why not *habitualise* routines so that that clutter becomes a distant memory?

And then what, you ask? Imagine how your home life will transform. So, grab your bin bags and get ready to declutter like you've never decluttered before!

DECLUTTERING YOUR HOME FOR MENTAL FOCUS AND EMOTIONAL WELL-BEING

THE DARK SIDE OF A CLUTTERED HOME

When you have clutter in your home, remember that decision fatigue leads to crap decisions, as we covered in Chapter 4. Every glance at the chaos prompts the thought, "I should tidy that…and that…and that," and before you know it, you're worn out before you reach the kitchen!

A study of American mothers revealed that those living in a home that was unfinished or cluttered had elevated cortisol levels—the stress hormone. They were constantly stuck in fight-or-flight mode and felt depressed throughout the day.[13] Not the ideal scenario if you're already feeling overwhelmed.

STEPS TO UNCLUTTER THE CLUTTER

Confronting clutter can seem like an overwhelming task. Let me ask you: have you ever felt paralyzed when faced with the decision to either keep or discard an item?

Marie Kondo, author of *The Life-Changing Magic of Tidying Up: The Japanese Art of Decluttering and Organizing*, suggests a straightforward approach: **hold each item and ask, "Does this spark joy?" If the answer is yes, keep it—otherwise discard it.**

She proposes decluttering your home by category, starting with clothes, then books, papers, miscellaneous items and leaving mementos last.

A successful strategy we've used in the past, is to tackle clutter room by room. Moreover, breaking down the task into specific areas within a room, such as a display cabinet. We've found this strategy helps us to experience a feeling of completion, as each zone or room serves as a milestone.

Thanking the item for its service before discarding it, can give you a sense of relief—especially if you feel guilty about letting go.

When assessing items, consider whether you've used them in the last twelve months. If you're keeping something "just in case" and it holds good resale value, then selling it on platforms like eBay or Craigslist can be lucrative.

You can think of eBay as a free storage locker. You sell it there, and then if you need the item again, you can re-buy it for about the same price you sold it for. Sarah and I have made over £1,000 in a weekend, selling our unused possessions on eBay.

For example, I used to have a Canon SLR camera with a couple of expensive lenses and an external flash. It was that classic mistake of having good intention to use it, but never taking it out with me as it was so heavy and bulky. The resolution on phones is so good these days, that my SLR never came out of its carry case—so I sold it.

Are you paying for a storage container? Evaluate the cost of maintaining a storage container over ten years, factoring in rental, time and travel. Is it more cost-effective to donate or sell the items instead?

To simplify the process of decluttering, we place a large bag in the hallway for items to give away. External family members get the first pick, and the remainder is donated to charity shops.

If you're overwhelmed by a mountain of clutter, then another suggestion is to discard three things from your house every day. Alternatively, you could outsource the decluttering by paying someone to do it for you, or with you.

Decluttering can be really draining when everything has emotional value to you. I experienced this going through my father's possessions after he passed away. In situations like that, I've found it good to have a supportive person with you, who can help you to decide the fate of the more difficult items.

In our family, we schedule decluttering sessions in the summer and before Christmas. We have a one-in-one-out policy for our kids' presents, to help maintain a tidy house.

However, books are one of our guilty pleasures, as we tend to read over 100 books per year. Our bookcase had books stacked in front of books! Eventually we donated all the ones we hadn't read for years and started buying digital books and borrowing from the library. While I still prefer the feeling of paper books, digital takes up no space at home.

Join the simplicity movement. Be conscious about what you buy. Consider value, joy, and prioritise experiences over stuff, to reduce clutter. For reference, revisit Chapter 5 and look at the section on

Simplifying Expenses. It will help you to make more mindful choices when buying things.

How Large a Home Do You Need?

Big houses cost more to buy, heat, maintain, and take more time to clean. As we grow older, we tend to stick to our routines and are resistant to change our environment. It's quite common to see an elderly person living in a four-bedroom house on her own, because she doesn't want to move.

Those empty bedrooms are costing you! If you're holding onto extra space for occasional visits from adult children, it's worth considering how many times a year will they really stay. Could you downsize to a more economical option and place a sofa bed in your lounge?

Location matters—are you living in the best place for you?

You can enhance the quality of your life by moving closer to work, or to your support network. We moved nearer to our parents so they could look after our kids during our weekly date day, plus the occasional overnight stay.

Fix Dissatisfiers in Your Home

It's time to fix those pesky dissatisfiers lurking in your home. You know, those things that make you annoyed or cringe every time you see them!

We learned in Chapter 4 that **fixing "Dissatisfiers" can bring more happiness than buying a new item.** As you walk through your home, become more aware when your mind is drawn to things that are broken, or you feel are repulsive.

When we moved into our current home, the room we chose as our office had dark, burnt-orange coloured walls. We spent a lot of time in our office, so every trip back from getting a cup of tea or a bathroom break, gave us a shot of dissatisfaction. It also didn't do us any favours on Zoom calls! Eventually we hit our breaking point, brushed on three coats of white paint, and voila—instant relaxation.

Fixing dissatisfiers can also apply to your kids! No, you can't swap your kids for a new one!

One of the common complaints I hear from other mothers is, "My kids don't lift a finger around the house!" Well, we're on a mission to teach our kids how to live independently. They put their plates by the sink after meals, wash and put away their clothes every week and clean their rooms. Sure, there's some moaning involved, but they're gradually getting used to looking after themselves. Our teenage daughter even cooks dinner for the whole family on occasion.

HABITUALISING WEEKLY ROUTINES

Sarah and I conquer the chaos of chores, by placing them as recurring events in our diary.

These include things such as bin collections, clothes washing, car cleaning, tyre pressure checks and mowing the lawn. We also diarise important renewals like car insurance. It's not sexy, but it gets things done.

And speaking of routines, Sarah and I have our set morning routine to nourish ourselves before our kids get up. Plus, we have our kids evening routine.

Now, wait a minute! Are you one of those parents doing Olympic-level shuttle runs to various clubs with your kids?

Picture this: I knew a mother with 4 kids. She picked them up after school and drove them all to separate clubs, while they ate their dinner in the car. This happened every school day. That's dedication. But you may find that kids would rather spend quality time with you instead.

So, turn your chores into victories and habitualise your routines.

The Magic of Lists

We streamline our travel preparations through packing lists. We have a document with everything to pack for a holiday with our kids. Each time we go away, we don't need to think much, we just print it off, and tick each item as we pack it. This saves time and the stress of realising we've forgotten something like a passport, or a kid's favourite toy.

I've moved home eleven times so far, and it won't be the last. Each time you move, there are so many companies to contact—banks, savings, pension, credit cards, utilities, driver's license, insurance, and so on. **We've got a moving list document** with over fifty companies to contact. Moving is stressful, so we keep our list updated, making it one thing we don't need to think about very much.

Separating Work and Home Life

Navigating the delicate dance of work and home life with kids is like trying to juggle flaming torches. We've been working from home for over eighteen years and have been burned a few times.

When we were in more conventional jobs, just the mere sight of our laptops was stressful. We had to set ourselves a curfew—no laptops or phones after a specific hour.

It's important not to continue working when your workday is over. There will always be more work to do—it's endless. Working in the evenings will worsen your sleep and make you a lot less productive the next day, as it reduces your decision capacity.

Remember, being busy does not mean you're producing effective results. It's well recognised that 20% of your efforts produce 80% of your results. Simplify and delete the busy work!

Simplicity Secret

Our previous house was much smaller. Picture our "L'office"—Lounge/Office. We had a TV and sofa at one end of the lounge, and two desks, filing cabinet and a printer at the other. We felt stressed every time we glanced at the work area in the evening. **Eventually we bought an inexpensive wooden screen and closed off the area at the end of the "work" day.**

Fast forward to the present, and we've ditched the 9-to-5 for an unconventional life. Our home office is not just for work that we pick up and put down—it's where we spend most of our time doing online training, video calls, managing our money, ordering groceries, Sarah's choir practice and writing books.

We don't book meetings after 5pm, as that's when we begin our kid's nightly routine, starting with dinner.

We've also thrown the conventional work hours out the window and embraced a seven-day work-life integration. We home educate our children, so days of the week are irrelevant. We prefer to go out during the week, when it's quieter. Our kids go to their grandparents once a week, so that Sarah and I can have a date day. We also go on holiday outside of the regular school holidays.

Striking a Balance with Technology

Picture this: Sarah and I used to waste an hour a week recording my appointments in her paper diary—and then recording her movements in my online diary. Believe me, it took some convincing to get Sarah to share my online calendar!

She'd be the first to admit that it's much simpler, now that we have a shared diary. Plus, we can access our shared diary from our phones and laptop, anywhere in the world.

We've assigned different colours to calendar events, such as: Sarah, me, both of us, and for the kids. It works really well to have the whole household in there, as it avoids scheduling conflicts. We also schedule meetings on days that we have to be in, so that we can free up days to go out. But as Uncle Ben said to Spider-Man Peter Parker, "With great power comes great responsibility." Sometimes I pop out and come back to find she's filled up my to do list!

Digital is the future—we're all raising the next generation of tech savvy kids. So, while we encourage our children to spend time on technology, we've created intentional boundaries for screen time.

In the morning, we have a rule that our kids must be ready before they can look at their phone or laptop. At dinnertime, we take away their computers and devices, so they can start to wind down for sleep. I'm certain that if we left them with their devices overnight, then they wouldn't go to sleep.

When I was a child, we'd go off running around a forest for hours on our own. These days, playing is all about online gaming. One tip to connect with your children is to play multi-player online games with them. They love it.

Interview: Jack Boken, Happy Jack Yoga

What was your life like before you embraced simplicity?

I used to have a really unhealthy and chaotic lifestyle. I was an alcoholic, I took crack cocaine and crystal meth and I weighed over 250 pounds. I was working in a corporate job at John Deere and was over $100,000 in debt from student loans, my wedding and a new car.

In 2009 I got divorced and finally got sober and came off the drugs. I also reduced my weight. By 2010 I'd taken the yoga teaching qualification and started holding yoga classes—and that's when things really started to change.

I realised how great I felt teaching yoga and decided this is what I wanted to do with my life. I didn't want to carry on sitting in a cubicle designing tractors anymore. I wanted to do something more meaningful, so I made a plan to tidy up my finances and leave in eighteen months. I wanted the freedom to see the world.

How did you prepare for this huge change to your life?

Yoga helped me to simplify my life. I went from living in a big countryside house in Iowa, to an apartment in Calgary. Then I downsized to a basement apartment—I didn't really care about fancy places at that point. And then eventually I moved back home with my parents.

I had split things 50/50 with my ex-wife, but in the end, I gave her all my furniture and my TV. It was so freeing to have nothing and start fresh. I'm not suggesting everybody needs to give up everything, but there was something so liberating about taking those steps and simplifying and downsizing.

By 2012 I'd finished my MBA and paid off my student loans. I'd also finalised my divorce. I wanted to make sure I'd tidied up all my affairs before I began travelling.

What happened when you left the corporate world to travel?

As soon as I quit my job, I took a one-way ticket to India. I knew I wanted to go to India because this was the birthplace of yoga.

I had all my possessions in a regular sized office backpack. It was hot in India, so I didn't need many clothes. All I packed was two pairs of shorts, boxers, socks and t-shirts. Plus, one pair of pants (trousers), one long sleeve shirt, a pair of shoes, toothbrush and toothpaste. I also had my passport, cash, credit card and a journal to write in.

It just felt so liberating to release everything. I didn't have a job or family and I barely had any stuff. It felt like I had no responsibility—no demands on me. All I had to do was find a place to eat, find a place to stay, and have enough money to take care of myself.

I was still teaching yoga in India. I'd often teach at an orphanage or school.

Living in India with no responsibilities gave me so much mental space. I wrote a lot in my journals and got clarity on what I wanted to do with my life.

What happened when you left India?

I lived in India for about a year and then moved back home with my parents in Canada. I wanted to fill my life with doing meaningful work, so I went full-time with my yoga teaching company—Happy Jack Yoga.

I still had the urge to travel, so I'd teach workshops and stay with friends. I'd go to Cleveland, then Seattle, California, Sacramento, Vancouver, Calgary. I also took cheap flights to Europe. I was still living pretty simply, with a backpack and a guitar. I felt like a rock star on tour.

Eventually I wanted to connect more with people and turned my business into an international yoga school, teaching regular people to become yoga instructors. I really love connecting with people—it fills my soul.

In 2013, I faced a significant challenge—I was diagnosed with cancer. The years of neglecting my body had caught up with me. However, fuelled by the newfound wisdom and motivation from my experiences in India and my dedication to yoga, I approached the diagnosis with resilience. Rather than dreading the treatment, I embraced it as an opportunity for healing and transformation.

How does simplicity affect your home life now?

I've been cancer free for ten years. I still have an attachment to financial security, so I still take a percentage of my paycheque and put it into growing my retirement fund. Having been at stages in my life where I've been overextended with loans, I don't want to slip up again.

I keep my life pretty simple now. After getting cancer I'm more aware of not pushing myself too hard. I'm craving that simple life again, so I'm moving into a local ashram for three months to give me time to reflect. I'll still be instructing yoga teachers online as usual, but I'll have more time in-between sessions to meditate and live simply.

FOLLOW JACK BOKEN:
Facebook: @HappyJackYoga
Instagram: @happyjackyoga
YouTube: @happyjackyoga
happyjackyoga.com

Get a FREE Complete Beginners Guide to Yoga and Meditation course with Happy Jack Yoga
bit.ly/ss-freeyoga

Conclusion: Home Life

The dark side of a cluttered home has been exposed, revealing the barriers to our peace and productivity. Uncluttering may seem daunting, but we've laid out steps that can turn the overwhelming task into a manageable feat.

We've learned it's not about the quantity of material things you own, it's about the quality and the joy each item brings. In Jack Boken's revealing interview, he shared insights on how little possessions we actually need for a fulfilling life.

Fixing dissatisfiers in your home is like weeding out negativity from your life garden. And just as a garden needs regular care, habitualising weekly routines ensures a clutter-free, stress-free environment. The small, consistent efforts compound into significant changes over time.

Now, separating the work from home life is crucial for maintaining balance and preserving your mental well-being. Technology is a double-edged sword. Striking a balance with online diaries and limiting screen time allows us to reclaim precious moments for ourselves and our loved ones.

CHAPTER 9

Simplify Health and Fitness

Disclaimer: Seek the advice of a medical professional and dietitian before making a change to your health and fitness, to ensure it is safe for your personal circumstances. Be sensible.

"If you have no health, you have no business."
— George Choy

INTRODUCTION

Health and fitness are a passion that's fuelled my journey since I was thirteen years old. I remember firstly lifting weights in my bedroom, then later moving my equipment to a shed in the garden, because my father was worried the weights would fall through the ceiling!

I have a thirst for knowledge, so in later years I became a Personal Trainer and Calisthenics instructor. In addition, Sarah and I are also certified Yoga and Meditation teachers.

However, let's not sugar coat health—life can throw you some major curveballs. For instance, in Chapter 5 on Money, we witnessed Diana Finch-Keran's life turn upside down, when her husband's health declined.

Health issues can happen at any time. During our children's junior school years (age 7-11), two mothers we knew passed away in their 40s, leaving behind devastated young families.

I also recall a sombre moment in my corporate life, when I'd heard a colleague had suffered a heart attack and died at his desk. Two other colleagues were on extended sick leave, battling work-related stress, anxiety, and depression. The average age of suicide is getting younger and younger each year. The rise of health issues is no longer exclusive to the elderly.

For those who have faced a significant medical diagnosis, or know someone who has, you'll understand that everything else immediately takes a back seat. **Health becomes the focal point of your family's universe—work, money, life, everything else becomes a lower priority.**

Medical issues were the reason we went on our personal journey to simplify our life—and later feeling compelled to write this book to help as many people as possible. In nearly every call we went on, people told us they needed to simplify their life.

Improving your health and fitness isn't a straightforward task—adding something new introduces complexity. **However, we've dissected the confusion to unveil scientifically proven, simple changes that will give you the biggest impact.**

This chapter is your guide to making health and fitness a habit, cutting through the noise of information and misinformation prevalent in the industry, due to commercial interests and the use of performance-enhancing drugs.

We'll make health and fitness simple by showing you a range of proven protocols like the Fantastic Four, the Daily Dozen, and the secrets of the centenarians living in the Blue Zone.

We'll also cover which types of exercise to do and how to make them a habit. You choose what works for best for you.

As we navigate this chapter, keep in mind the Simplicity Secret Tool:

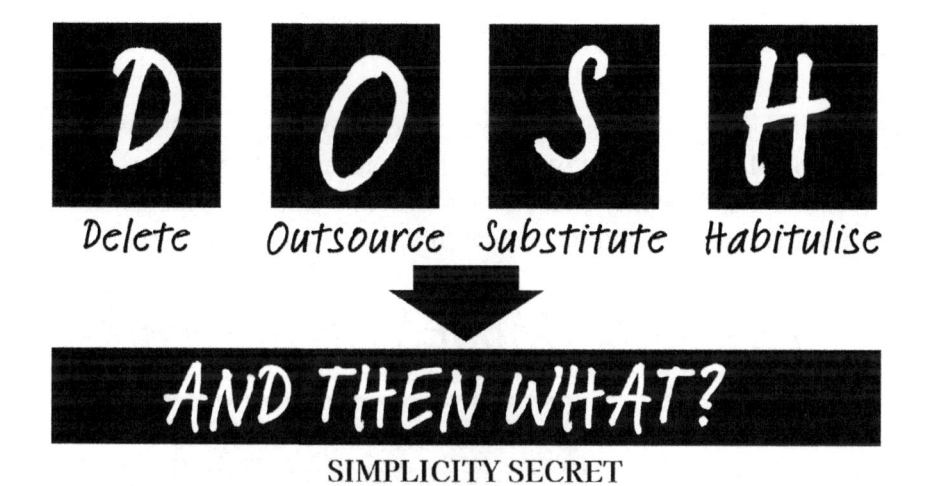

D Delete   **O** Outsource   **S** Substitute   **H** Habitulise

AND THEN WHAT?

SIMPLICITY SECRET

Will you *delete* that waist busting processed food from your cupboards and *substitute* them for healthy choices?

Will you *outsource* your fitness, and *habitualise* it into your life?

The decision lies with you. Your health isn't primarily dictated by your genes—it's mostly shaped by the food and lifestyle choices you make.

SIMPLIFYING YOUR DIET FOR A LONG LIFE

WHAT'S GOING TO GET YOU?

Despite the gloomy statistics below, according to Boston University School of Medicine, most of the leading causes of death are preventable, and mainly caused by we eat and drink.[14] Diet is also the number one contributor to disability.[15]

LEADING CAUSES OF DEATH

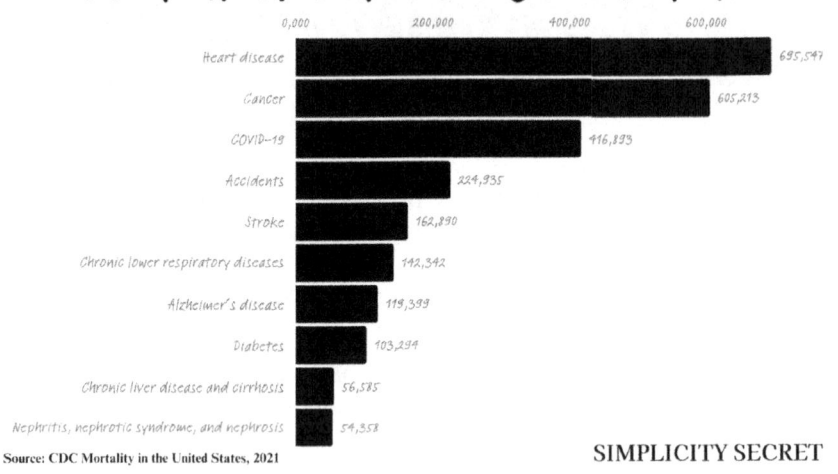

Cause	Deaths
Heart disease	695,547
Cancer	605,213
COVID-19	416,893
Accidents	224,935
Stroke	162,890
Chronic lower respiratory diseases	142,342
Alzheimer's disease	119,399
Diabetes	103,294
Chronic liver disease and cirrhosis	56,585
Nephritis, nephrotic syndrome, and nephrosis	54,358

Source: CDC Mortality in the United States, 2021

Rather than succumbing to this grim news, there's a silver lining—**you hold the key to averting or even reversing these ailments within your body.** By making simple adjustments to your diet, you'll not only lengthen your lifespan, but also embrace vibrant health.

From Vanity to Vitality: My Journey from the Brink of a Heart Attack

Picture this: I'd gone to a doctor's clinic for a regular check-up. I was in my forties, wearing a tank top, looking lean and muscular. I appeared to be in perfect health and fitness. I sat on a chair as the nurse put the blood pressure cuff around my arm. The nurse leaned in, "You're going to ace this one!"

A few minutes later, she looked alarmed, "Oh, that's not right." She tested it again. **My blood pressure was sky high!** She asked me to come back again in a week for a re-test.

A week later, they couldn't believe it was still so high—I mean I looked so fit! They scheduled in multiple blood pressure tests over several days and weeks.

In the meantime, I had blood drawn to test my cholesterol levels. Later I got the results. You know those charts you see with a minimum and maximum level? **Well, my reading was way off the chart at around fifty percent above the maximum level.** It finally dawned on me that looking good didn't always lead to being healthy—I wanted both.

Sarah was worried. I was even more worried, as unknown to her and my two toddlers I was hiding a dark secret.

For the last few weeks my heart would stop beating for a second, multiple times a day. I never knew whether my next breath would be my last. It felt like something clogged it and then got unstuck again. I imagined being another digit on the chart of deaths due to heart disease.

At the time, I never considered "And then what?"

How would Sarah and my two toddlers cope with my death?

How would it affect our finances?

Have I got my affairs in order?

I never considered any of these things.

The only thing I was concerned about was being placed on medication...forever. I had a fear of medications after witnessing my late father on a myriad of drugs, with escalating side effects. Medications seemed like an endless downward spiral.

Both America and the UK's number one killer is heart disease. It results from fatty cholesterol-rich gunk being deposited in the walls of your arteries. It restricts the blood flow to your heart and can eventually lead to a heart attack.

Not only that, but if the heart attack doesn't kill you, research by Harris in 2010, concluded that **there's a growing body of evidence showing a link between cholesterol levels and Alzheimer's disease.**[16]

One of my friends suggested reading a book on plant-based eating. I was a big meat eater at the time and ate reasonably high fat foods. The thought of eating a plant-based diet seemed extreme to me. But more extreme is having your chest cracked open for a heart bypass.

For over 35 years, Dean Ornish M.D. and others have been reversing heart disease through diet and lifestyle changes. In one of his studies published in The Journal of the American Medical Association, **there was a 91% reduction in anginal episodes with patients placed on a low fat, whole foods plant-based diet.**[17]

Although initially sceptical as a meat enthusiast, I embraced the challenge, transitioning to a 100% whole foods plant-based diet over a weekend.

The first thought to cross my mind was, "Where do I get my protein?"

I discovered you can get more than enough protein by switching meat for beans, lentils, tofu and tempeh. I was also worried about losing muscle mass, but quickly discovered there were plenty of plant-based bodybuilders and strongmen, showing that you can build muscle eating only plants. Gorillas have a huge muscle mass and only 3% of their diet is meat—the rest is plants.

What were my results? After three weeks my blood pressure returned to normal levels. After three months my dangerously high cholesterol levels were now in the middle of the healthy range. I recovered faster from exercise and best of all, **the haunting moments of impending heart attacks vanished.**

Sarah also ate plant-based with me and managed to reverse some arthritis in her hand, and the chronic constipation she had suffered since she was 18. TMI, I admit—but you come to appreciate the basic body functions when they haven't worked properly your entire adult life!

My intent isn't to persuade you to adopt a fully plant-based diet, just to share my journey and make you aware that looking fit doesn't always mean you are healthy. Choose what aligns with your values and get regular check-ups with your doctor.

Okay, let's move onto some scientifically proven protocols to help you massively improve your health.

The Fantastic Four

A study involving over 23,000 participants revealed that adhering to just four healthy lifestyle factors, reduced the likelihood of diabetes, heart attacks, stroke, and cancer over 7.8 years by a whopping 78%.[18]

The four factors:

1. Never smoking
2. Having a body mass index (BMI) below 30
3. Performing 30 minutes of physical activity per day
4. Eating predominately fruit, vegetables and whole grains, with low consumption of meat.

That's a straightforward formula for a longer and healthier life.

Simply replace meat in a few of your meals with beans, lentils, chickpeas, hummus, tofu, tempeh, or other soy products.

The Daily Dozen

Developed by Michael Greger M.D. of NutritionFacts.org and author of *How Not To Die, How Not To Diet,* and *How Not To Age.*

The Daily Dozen is an amazing checklist of the healthiest foods to eat—unlocking a healthier, disease-resistant life. These twelve powerhouse foods, each supported by multiple studies, are your ticket to vitality.

You can download the Daily Dozen checklist app at the end of this section. Don't sweat it if you can't tick off everything each day—just achieving some of them can still be a game-changer for your health.

1. Legumes
Beans / Lentils / Chickpeas / Hummus / Tofu / Tempeh / Soy
3 servings per day
Serving: ½ cup cooked legumes or ¼ cup of hummus

Legumes are your plant-based protein pals—an alternative for meat in your meals.

One of the preventative cancer recommendations in a paper produced by the World Cancer Research Fund, together with the American Institute for Cancer Research, was that people should "Eat relatively unprocessed cereals (grains) and/or pulses (legumes) with every meal."

One of the other benefits of legumes, is they can help you lose weight. How does that work? Well, legumes have an extremely low glycaemic index and **can reduce the blood sugar rush from eating high glycaemic foods in the same meal.**

However, what may be lesser known, **is that legumes also have a "second-meal effect," benefiting people many hours later.** A study of participants given legumes for dinner, not only experienced reduced blood sugar in the meal they were eating, but also experienced a reduction in expected blood sugar levels the next morning—even when they ate a sugary breakfast.[19] This side-effect is caused by the friendly gut bacteria that love legumes.

I use canned beans, rather than preparing them from dry beans, as they take a long time to cook. Red lentil pasta is another tasty and easy option.

Please note that it takes a couple of weeks for your gut bacteria to ramp up to process legumes, so increase them slowly. The easiest to digest are tofu, lentils, canned adzuki beans, mung beans and chickpeas.

2. Berries
1 serving per day
Serving: ½ cup fresh or frozen, or ¼ cup dried

Berries are a superfood, packing nearly ten times more antioxidants than other fruits and vegetables. They can protect you against cancer, boost your immune system, and protect your liver. One serving keeps the doctor away.

3. Other Fruits
3 servings per day
Serving: 1 medium fruit or ¼ cup dried fruit

Variety is the spice of life. Each have their own benefits to your health. Three servings a day will load you up with antioxidants and phytonutrients.

A study of over 187,000 people found that greater consumption of whole fruits was significantly associated with a lower risk of type 2 diabetes.[20]

However, watch out for fruit juices, as removing the pulp puts you at risk for type 2 diabetes.

4. Cruciferous Vegetables
Brussel Sprouts / Rocket / Arugula / Bok Choy / Cabbage / Cauliflower / Broccoli / Kale / Radishes
1 serving a day
Serving: ½ cup

Cruciferous vegetables can potentially prevent breast cancer, prostate cancer, boost liver detox enzymes, protect your brain, eyesight, and manage type 2 diabetes.

A meta-analysis study encompassing over 1.2 million people across 35 studies, found that a high intake of cruciferous vegetables significantly reduced your risk of colorectal cancer.[21]

One study of autistic participants, found that 2-3 servings a day of cruciferous vegetables resulted in significant improvements in social interaction, abnormal behaviour, and verbal communication within weeks.[22]

5. Leafy Greens
Rocket / Arugula / Kale / Spinach / Lettuce / Coriander / Cilantro / and many more
2 servings per day
Serving: 1 cup raw, ½ cup cooked

These nitrate rich heroes help reduce blood pressure and lower your risk of heart disease.[23]

One word of warning—if you're on blood thinners like warfarin then speak to your medical doctor first, as the interaction of greens and blood thinners can result in death.

6. Other Vegetables
Carrots / Asparagus / Bell Peppers / Corn / Pumpkin / Potatoes / Squash / Courgette / Zucchini / and many more
Eat a wide variety
2 servings
Serving: ½ cup

An article published in Nature Medicine concluded that increasing vegetable consumption led to a reduction in the risk of strokes and oesophageal cancer.[24]

7. Ground Flaxseeds
1 serving: 1 Tablespoon

Flaxseeds are high in omega-3 fatty acids. In a 6-month study, taking flaxseed versus a placebo each day resulted in a significant reduction in blood pressure.[25] And as the world's oceans are polluted with mercury, leading to brain and nervous system issues—flaxseeds can be a safer choice than some sources of high omega-3 seafood.

One study concluded that there is convincing evidence that milled flaxseed improves cardiovascular disease, cancer, gut health and diabetes.[26]

When you buy flaxseeds, make sure they are ground, otherwise you can't absorb the nutrients. I mostly stir it in my porridge/oatmeal or blend it in a smoothie bowl. You can also sprinkle it on your food.

8. Nuts and Seeds
1 serving per day
Serving: ¼ cup nuts or seeds. 2 Tablespoons nut or seed butter

Research by Loma Linda University concluded that the risk of coronary heart disease is 37% lower for those consuming nuts more than four times per week.[27]

9. Herbs and Spices
1 serving per day: up to ¼ teaspoon

There are so many herbs and spices. Each one is like a concentrated superfood. I tend to put quite a few in my breakfast. I add turmeric with black pepper for inflammation, Ceylon Cinnamon to improve blood sugar levels, Cocoa powder to improve artery function and mood, ginger to reduce muscle pain, migraines and potentially assist weight loss. If you're on medication then check with your medical doctor before introducing new herbs and spices every day.

10. Whole Grains
Barley / Buckwheat / Oats / Quinoa / Rye / Whole wheat pasta
3 Servings per day
Serving: ½ cup cooked cereal. 1 slice of whole grain bread

Research investigating over 188,000 participants concluded that higher whole grain consumption significantly reduced the risk of heart disease.[28]

11. Beverages
Water, tea, coffee

Drink five to twelve glasses a day to substantially reduce your risk of a fatal heart attack.

It's worth mentioning a few benefits of the various hot liquids. Coffee can protect the liver[29], but I'd recommend not drinking more than three cups in the morning, as it negatively affects deep sleep and increases anxiety. A quarter of the caffeine is still in your system 10-12 hours after you drink it, so keep that in mind for your daily cut off point. If you have high blood pressure, then it would be preferable to eliminate or significantly reduce your caffeine intake.

Green tea, Jasmine green tea and Matcha can assist weight loss.[30] Hibiscus tea can lower blood pressure.[31]

12. Exercise
20 - 90 minutes of exercise per day. You can break it up into micro-doses.

Walking 20 minutes per day can reduce your chance of death by 7%, 40 minutes is twice as good at 14%[32] and 60 minutes may reduce the chance of death by 24%.[33]

13. Vitamin B12 (yes, I know it's more than a dozen)
Vitamin B12 is not made by plants or animals, but by microbes in the soil. Unfortunately, we don't get much natural B12 anymore. B12 deficiency can lead to disease or even death.

Animals often receive B12 supplements, so if you're a meat eater then you may already be receiving enough. You don't have to eat fully plant based to do the daily dozen. But if you decide to mostly eat plant-based, then it is non-negotiable to take a good B12 supplement. Dr Greger recommends taking 2,000 micrograms of B12 cyanocobalamin once a week, or 50 micrograms daily.

There you have it, your Daily Dozen for a life that's not just lived, but in vibrant health:

1. Legumes

2. Berries

3. Other Fruits

4. Cruciferous Vegetables

5. Leafy Greens

6. Other Vegetables

7. Ground Flaxseeds

8. Nuts and Seeds

9. Herbs and Spices

10. Whole Grains

11. Beverages

12. Exercise

Plus a Vitamin B12 supplement if you decide to mostly trade meat for plant-based options.

There's a **handy free app** you can download to check off the daily dozen:
bit.ly/ss-dozen

THE SECRET TO LIVE TO 100: BLUE ZONES

There are so many diet styles in the world—and heck, I've tried most of them in the past. **They all feel they can fully justify why theirs is the best and most healthy diet.**

The only problem is, very few have been tested long-term to see whether they positively, or negatively affect your health. **Wouldn't it be better to work backwards, by looking for the longest-lived and healthiest people instead? Enter the Blue Zones.**

Blue Zones was first coined by Dan Buettner, author of *The Blue Zones 2nd Edition: 9 Lessons for Living Longer from the People Who've Lived the Longest.*

Dan travelled with a team of scientists to identify global hotspots where individuals not only reached the remarkable age of 100, but also enjoyed a high quality of life in their later years. They used a blue marker pen to designate areas with an unusually high number of centenarians, and the name stuck.

These centenarians were also very active and in great physical health—many of them were still working.

The original Blue Zone explorations showing the highest concentrations of centenarians were in five locations:

- Loma Linda, California, USA
- Ikaria, Greece
- Barbagia region of Sardinia, Italy
- Okinawa, Japan
- Nicoya Peninsula, Costa Rica

For those of us following a Western diet, it's truly fascinating to see USA's Loma Linda on the list. The residents there are outliving people just a few miles away, as well as the rest of the country—proving that both your diet and lifestyle can significantly impact your lifespan.

The Blue Zones team comprised of medical researchers, anthropologists, demographers, and epidemiologists. They searched for evidence-based secrets to longevity. The secrets went beyond diet and exercise. What did they all have in common?

They referred to them as the Power 9®

1. Move Naturally

Most of the centenarians didn't do formal exercise. Instead, they were active most of their day. They would be gardening, collecting food and kneading bread. Many were shepherds hiking for miles each day. They continued working after reaching our typical western retirement age.

The exception to the activity rule was Loma Linda, based in the United States. They did more organised based activities in addition to gardening and housework, such as hiking, community sports, yoga, tai chi, swimming, dancing and strength training.

2. Purpose

This is why you get out of bed in the morning. **Many of the Blue Zone centenarians were still working in their jobs or volunteering in their community.** Others were helping look after grandchildren and great grandchildren.

Outside of the Blue Zones, **feeling that you have a strong sense of purpose has been shown to extend your life**, regardless of how old you are.

A 14-year study by Patrick Hill of Carleton University in Canada concluded[34], *"Our findings point to the fact that finding a direction for life, and setting overarching goals for what you want to achieve can help you actually live longer."*

Moreover, *"So the earlier someone comes to a direction for life, the earlier these protective effects may be able to occur."*

If you'd like to deep dive into finding your purpose, then take a look at one of our other books:

Find Your Purpose: A Practical Guide for Discovering Your Purpose and Creating a Life You Love
bit.ly/fypurpose

3. Downshift

People in the Blue Zones still experience stress. High levels of stress lead to chronic inflammation and can lead to many diseases.

We believe stress is what caused Sarah and I to have our recent medical diagnosis. Since then, we've taken substantial steps to reduce stress in our life. Meditation is just one of the many tools we use.

To combat stress in the Blue Zones, they regularly set aside downtime. The Sardinians and Nicoyans rest and socialise with friends in the afternoon. The Okinawans take a few moments each day to remember their ancestors.

The people in Loma Linda pray each day, and from sunset on Friday to sunset on Saturday, they create a sanctuary where they don't work and focus all their time on their families, nature, and God.

4. 80% Rule

The Okinawans stop eating when their stomachs are 80% full. This ensures they maintain a lean weight all year round.

Most of the Blue Zones also eat more at breakfast and lunch, then have their smallest meal for dinner.

As the saying goes, "Breakfast like a king; lunch like a prince; dinner like a pauper."

5. Plant Slant

The centenarian diet was mostly beans and lentils instead of meat—providing life extending and disease protecting properties. On average, they only ate a piece of meat around the size of a deck of cards, once a week.

6. Wine @ 5

Perhaps controversial, but the centenarians tended to drink 1-2 glasses of wine per day with food, in the company of friends or family. The exception was in Loma Linda, where they didn't drink.

7. Belong

Nearly all the centenarians interviewed belonged to a faith-based community. It didn't matter what religion it was. The sense of belonging increased their connection to others.

One study found that attending a religious service at least once a month reduced your risk of death by 20-30%.[35]

8. Loved Ones First

They were often living in multi-generational houses, with grandparents, parents and children together. Having a partner can add up to three years to your life. In addition, the children were more likely to care for their parents, after experiencing their parents doing it for grandparents.

9. Right Tribe

It has been known for many years that loneliness kills. This has increased since the pandemic.

The centenarians all belonged to social circles. The Okinawans went one step further to create "moais"—a group of five friends committed to each other for life. They were like a second family. They helped each other by pooling resources.

A study on loneliness and social isolation found that it reduced your life expectancy and increased psychological distress such as depression.[36]

So, that's the Blue Zone's secret to living to 100 years old with vitality—the Power 9®

1. Move Naturally
2. Purpose
3. Downshift
4. 80% Rule
5. Plant Slant
6. Wine @ 5
7. Belong
8. Loved Ones First
9. Right Tribe

Sarah's simple Weight Loss

Now, let's address processed foods. My wife Sarah used to be overweight. One day she found herself at her lowest point after seeing a photo of herself. She hated the way her thighs rubbed together and felt disgusted about herself. On that day, she made a commitment to shed the extra pounds.

Her approach? Only eat whole foods and lift weights. Simple. Sarah lost 56 pounds by doing that.

So out went the cookies, cakes, desserts, chips, crisps, burgers, bread, ready meals and fast food. We stocked up on whole food—this is food close to its natural state.

Whatever your chosen dietary path, we've found that the quickest way to reduce body fat is to eliminate processed food.

Packed with calories and often loaded with flavour enhancers, these culprits keep you craving for more. **Replace them with whole foods for more volume with fewer calories.** There are some exceptions of healthy processed food you can include, such as yogurt, tofu, tempeh and steel cut oats.

Consider the daily calorie target: 2,000 calories for women and 2,500 for men. Now, contemplate a typical fast-food burger meal—1,100 to 1,500 calories. That's nearly three-quarters of your daily intake! That seemingly innocent coffee shop muffin adds another 500 calories, eclipsing your daily limit. Processed foods are condensed calories—they may not fill your stomach, but they pack a calorific punch and leave you hungry for more.

Food can be very addictive; some people are more susceptible than others. If you think that you need more support handling your relationship with food, look into support groups such as Overeaters Anonymous, or Bright Line Eating®. Sarah tried both and found the scientific and psychological approach in Bright Line Eating® extremely helpful in losing and maintaining the weight loss.

LOSE WEIGHT WITH A TIDY KITCHEN

Remember our discussion on decision fatigue in Chapter 4? A cluttered kitchen is also bad for your waistline. A Cornell University study discovered that individuals placed in a chaotic kitchen, ate more than twice as many cookies as those in a tidy kitchen.[37]

HABITUALISE YOUR MEALS

Simplify your approach to health and waistline by habitualising your meals. **Choose a few go-to meals**, perhaps rotating between two breakfast options based on your workout routine—that's what I do.

Make your lunch consistent and limit your dinner to a handful of reliable choices. Embrace bulk cooking on weekends, freezing portions for effortless meals after work. Less thinking equals more success.

Consider implementing a rule, like avoiding restaurants and takeout for a month. Habitualising your meals makes the journey smoother. **Also, habitualise the timing of your meals**—your body loves routine.

Monitoring Your Health

The widely used BMI targets are flawed, as they take no account of how much muscle you have. **A superior approach involves buying inexpensive bathroom scales with the capability to measure your body fat**, and also your muscle mass. They aren't as accurate as an expensive DEXA scan, but they are significantly better than just tracking your weight. Many of these scales sync with your phone for easy tracking of your progress.

Alternatively, if you're not ready to splurge on new scales, calculate your waist-to-height ratio by dividing your height in inches or centimetres by your waist measurement:

0.4 – 0.49 Low risk
0.5 – 0.59 Moderate risk
0.6+   High risk

I've found that my waist measurement always increases when I'm gaining fat.

Considering that the number one cause of death is heart disease, investing in an upper arm blood pressure monitor provides an easy way to monitor your health. Consistently high blood pressure can lead to severe health issues such as heart attacks, strokes, kidney disease, and dementia.

My wife Sarah and I document our results in a spreadsheet every month to track changes over time. This approach helps us to be aware of any issues early on. If you have high blood pressure, then refer back to the previous section, where we explored various dietary choices to help lower blood pressure.

Target blood pressure readings:

mmHg	**Result**
89/59 or lower	Low
90/60 to 120/80	Normal
135/85 to 140/90	High

If your blood pressure is consistently high, then medication could become necessary...which maybe for life unless you make substantial changes to your diet and lifestyle. Reducing salt and making sure you're drinking enough water can also help.

Habitualise Your Fitness Routine

Activities for Daily Living

We've seen in the research listed in this chapter, that **you can add substantial years to your life in as little as 20 minutes activity per day.** Ninety minutes is even better.

We've learned that the centenarians in the Blue Zones get most of their physical activity from daily living—whether that's gardening, making food from scratch, or still working in a physical job.

Take a look at your life to see whether there are ways you could incorporate movement into your day—perhaps walking instead of driving and taking the stairs instead of the elevator.

Pick Activities You Enjoy

In the vibrant lifestyles of the Blue Zones centenarians, longevity isn't tied to a specific workout regimen, but thrives on daily physical activity.

What's your passion? There's a variety of choices—swimming, dancing, hiking, martial arts, tai chi, tennis, table tennis, golf, basketball, baseball, roller skating, ice skating, skateboarding, rock climbing, frisbee, calisthenics, weightlifting, or yoga. **By choosing activities that ignite your passion, you're much more likely to exercise consistently.**

One thing that ensures Sarah and I exercise regularly, is to block it out in the diary. Having an appointment with a trainer, booking a weekly class or just having a regular routine, will automate it and make it easier to get into a good exercise habit.

Essential for Survival: Preserve Muscle

Have you ever noticed how toned and lean the people in their twenties usually look?

Much of it is due to their higher muscle mass. Muscle burns a lot more calories at rest, so it stokes your metabolism. Muscle also takes up a lot less space than fat, which is why you can stay the same weight for years, while steadily becoming fatter. A pound of fat is about the size of a grapefruit, whereas a pound of muscle is around the size of a tangerine. Muscle also loves to suck up carbohydrates after a resistance training session.

There's a downside to not doing resistance training. Age-related muscle loss, known as "sarcopenia," starts from the age of 30. If you don't lift heavy things, you can anticipate losing 3-5% of your muscle mass every decade. By the time you reach your 80s, you may have lost up to 50% of your muscle, leading to falls, fractures, insulin resistance, obesity and even death.[38]

Most people in the western world lack the strength to get out of a chair without using their hands as they age. They also can't squat to the floor.

Even if you believe you are 100% healthy now, according to the CDC, accidents are the fourth leading cause of death. Accidents are unpredictable. In a study of ICU patients, those with more muscle mass had lower rates of hospital death, and a higher rate of survival after they left.[39]

Conversely in the Blue Zones, the centenarians are doing strength training as part of their activities for daily living. A great example is the 100-year-old shepherds walking while carrying two heavy pails of milk from his cows. Or lifting stones to make rock walls.

In the western world, we don't tend to have jobs like this, so it's beneficial to add regular sessions of *resistance training* to your weekly activities. Many of the yogis I know lift weights and do yoga—the perfect synergy of strength and flexibility.

Resistance Training Simplified

In a nutshell, resistance training is anything done with load. You can either lift weights, heavy objects, or do calisthenics (body weight training).

I'm qualified to teach both calisthenics and weights, although I'm no longer taking on clients. Here are a few guidelines from my real-world experience of personal training men and women to get stronger.

1. How frequently to train?

Most of the bodybuilders of today, and many movie stars gaining 30 pounds of muscle in a few months for a film, **take some kind of steroid or other performance enhancing drug.** These drugs enable them to do huge volumes of training and exercise every day, packing on large amounts of muscle. **Natural gym goers like us make little to no progress on their routines.** It just leads to overtraining, injuries and little improvement from year to year.

What I love to do is to look back at the natural, professional bodybuilders in the pre-steroid era of the 1940s and 50s. **They predominantly did a full-body workout, three times per week.** For example, Monday, Wednesday and Friday. That gives your muscles a full 48 hours to rest and rebuild between workouts. In between you can walk, do yoga or play sports, as long as you avoid heavy lifting.

If you have less time, you can still maintain your muscle and make some strength gains, while lifting weights only once or twice a week. But it's not as effective as three times. However, see how your body responds. Many of the women I trained made huge jumps in their strength levels from training with me only twice a week.

Some people can handle more sets per body part by lifting four times per week, such as Monday, Tuesday, Thursday, Friday—splitting the body into two or three parts and increasing the number of sets. **However, I'm not genetically gifted enough to recover from that much volume.**

Keep your workouts between 20-60 minutes.

2. Don't injure yourself

This is my biggest rule. It's easy to get into a cycle of injuring yourself every couple of weeks. That results in you barely making any progress.

I've found that the biggest cause of injury is repetition (rep) speed, resulting in poor form.

If you move the weight at an explosive speed, then you tend to shift the work to muscles you shouldn't be using, and there's a point where the force is huge. To avoid this problem, take a minimum of one full second to raise the weight and the same to lower it. You can slowly say "one Mississippi" in your head as you move the weight.

If you have an existing injury, or movement in a specific position causes pain, then find an alternative exercise that works the same muscle but results in no discomfort at all.

Keep in mind that we're all built differently. Having a session with a Personal Trainer can help you to discover which exercises are better suited to your body and posture.

Finally, if you haven't done a specific exercise to failure in the last 7 days, then I recommend only doing half as many reps on your next workout.

I know you can do a lot more, but this tip will substantially cut down the soreness. You can aim for 75% on the second workout and 100% by the third workout. As they say in the military special forces, "slow is smooth and smooth is fast."

Burn Fat in Your Sleep

How much would you pay for a magic pill that builds your willpower reserves, improves mood, increases focus, burns fat, grows muscles, kills disease and extends your life?

Well, that magic pill comes from getting enough sleep—and best of all, it's free.

How Much Sleep to Burn Fat?

In a weight loss study conducted on two groups on a calorie restricted diet, one group slept for 8.5 hours and the other for only 5.5 hours.

The people with short sleep lost 55% less bodyfat and lost more muscle than those who slept for 8.5 hours.[40]

Not only that, but the short sleep group had elevated levels of the hormone ghrelin—known as the hunger hormone. If they weren't on a calorie-controlled diet, it is likely they would have eaten a lot more food!

Most people assume that you burn more calories when you are awake longer, but that's not the case. **When you're sleep deprived, your body reduces your metabolic rate—burning less calories to preserve energy.** The study estimated that the participants sleeping 3 hours less, burned 400 calories less per day.

What Time to Sleep?

In addition to how long you sleep, the time you go to bed also matters. In a study of 136,652 participants, they found that **going to bed between 8-10pm resulted in less obesity than going to bed later.**

Ben Franklin was onto something when he said, *"Early to bed, and early to rise, makes a man healthy, wealthy, and wise."*

5 Steps to Improve Your Sleep

1. Go to bed at the same time:
Your body likes routine. Go to bed and wake at the same time every day. If you're tired, go to bed even earlier that night, or take a nap during the day. Getting up later is not as healthy for you.

We've included a Yoga Nidra (yogic nap) meditation for a quick nap and brain break in the Bonus Content area of Chapter 2. You'll come back energised to carry on your day: bit.ly/ss-bonus-content

2. Sleep in the dark:
Have heavy curtains or black out blinds. Sit in low lighting in those 2-3 hours before sleep. Avoid turning on bright lights as they make you more alert. If you're very sensitive to light, you can wear blue light blocking glasses in those last 3 hours before sleep.

3. Zone out:
Avoid looking at your phone, email, work, or anything which could be distressing for at least 1½ hours before sleep. Spend time with your family, watch your guilty pleasures on TV, or read a book that doesn't require much brainpower.

4. Limit caffeine and keep it to the morning:
Caffeine can stay in your system for up to 12 hours, affecting sleep length. One study showed that consuming caffeine within 6 hours of your bedtime resulted in 1 hour less sleep.[41] Personally, I drink 2-3 cups of coffee early in the morning and none after that.

5. Limit alcohol:
Drinking alcohol at night results in less deep sleep. I've personally noticed I don't dream as much when I've had a couple of glasses of wine.

Conclusion: Health and Fitness

Understanding the leading causes of death is the first step towards taking control over your health. My journey from the brink of a heart attack serves as a powerful reminder that change is not only possible, but imperative. Proper nutrition, regular exercise, and sufficient sleep form the foundation of a vibrant life.

Implementing the Daily Dozen or embracing the secrets of centenarians in the Blue Zones, and learning to monitor your health, are essential practices that can add many years to your life.

Eating whole food, as highlighted in Sarah's weight loss journey, and maintaining a tidy kitchen, can transform your weight.

Habitualising your meals and fitness routine, reinforces positive behaviours, while activities for daily living and exercising for enjoyment, can make the journey towards health more fun.

Preserving muscle through resistance training and understanding the nuances of burning fat in your sleep, can make you healthier, live longer, and enjoy a better quality of life.

Your health is an investment, and by integrating these habits into your life, you're not just extending your life, but thriving with vitality!

CHAPTER 10

Tools to Reduce Overwhelm and Stress

INTRODUCTION

In this chapter, we'll give you the key tools to rapidly reduce stress, including the art of expressing your feelings, embracing the science of hugs, delving into meditation, letting go of suffering and exploring the transformative realm of yogic breathwork. Plus, there's a surprising discovery about gaming.

In the primal days, our ancestors encountered stress in the form of an attacker, such as a rival tribe or wild animal, triggering a fight-or-flight response. Today, it's unexpected bills, business issues, demanding bosses, conflicts with colleagues, emails, and family and friends that set our stress response in motion.

Modern life imposes obligations and societal norms, preventing us from unleashing our primal instincts. The result? **A mounting pile of unresolved "stress cycles," leading to anger, despair and depression**. We can't do what we've been programmed to do—to raise our fists and fight them or run for our lives. Sometimes we lose all hope, curl up into a ball and shut down. Our life goes up in flames around us and we fall into depression.

Our days are filled with these stress cycles and they never get completed—we just add another to the mountainous pile.

You can "complete the stress cycle" by engaging in physical activity, as highlighted in Chapter 9 on Health and Fitness. Giving your body the signal that you are "fighting or fleeing" will allow it to relax, as you have evaded the beast and are okay to resume normal life.

Whether it's lifting weights, kettlebell swings, boxing, running or dancing, physical activity is a powerful stressbuster. Incorporating vigorous activity into your daily routine, keeps you one step ahead of the stress avalanche. **You could just put on some music and dance to one song—shake it off!**

As an example: at the end of her workday, Sarah Beth from Sarah Beth Yoga likes to break the stress cycle, by either dancing or doing yoga to just one song.

Later in this chapter, we'll enter the world of yogic breathwork—your secret weapon against stress. Learn the art of effective breathing in this chapter to downregulate the stress response in minutes.

We'll learn how meditation expands your window of tolerance to stress, while the act of letting go releases stress as it arises. You'll recognise the end of the stress cycle when you feel relaxed again.

So, let's dive into these transformative practices and reclaim bliss, in the midst of life's chaos.

Embrace Daily Nurturing

We're all familiar with the pre-flight announcement to "secure your own oxygen mask before assisting others." Yet, in the realm of self-care, the key is to use these stress-relieving practices daily, not just when a crisis arises. **Daily nurturing helps you to build your emotional muscle so you're better prepared when a stressful event happens.**

It really helps to schedule specific, uninterrupted moments in your day for nurture time. Begin with modest goals, as building habits takes time.

Personally, Sarah and I cherish our nurture time during the peaceful hours of 5-7 am, before our kids get up. My daily self-care regimen involves journaling, exercise, pranayama (yogic breathwork), and meditation. I also read or watch something educational during this dedicated time.

One effective technique for reinforcing habits is "event stacking." It's easy to integrate a new habit, by either substituting it for an existing one, or combining it with a regular activity. For instance, consider waking up, briefly visiting the bathroom, then returning to bed for meditation. Alternatively, take a brisk 20-minute walk immediately after lunch every day.

You can compile a separate list of activities that bring you joy. This proves invaluable when you're feeling low or bored. Whether it's meditation, a leisurely bath, a walk in nature, chanting mantra, reading a novel, singing, jogging, weightlifting, playing video games, or baking—have a repertoire of instant, home-based activities you can turn to.

What nurtures YOUR soul may not nurture mine—this list should be tailored to what uplifts and fulfils YOU.

Also ask yourself which habits are not serving you. One of my previous habits was to link the event of putting my kids to bed with having a large glass of wine. This happened nearly every night for three years! Eventually I substituted the wine for a hot mug of jasmine green tea and broke the habit.

EXPRESS YOUR FEELINGS

Pour your unfiltered thoughts onto paper in a journal, or open up to your partner, friend or family member. The act of sharing helps release pent-up stressful thoughts.

Remember, if the burden becomes too great, seek guidance from a mental health professional. Also, consider phoning an anonymous 24-hour hotline such as 116 123 (Samaritans) in the UK, or 988 (Lifeline) in the USA for immediate support.

I used to bottle up my feelings and not talk to anyone about them—so believe me when I say I know how difficult this is. After a number of potentially life-threatening issues, I've committed to be more open with Sarah. We have regular time scheduled each day where we can discuss not only what's bothering us, but also anything uplifting.

Hug It Out

One study found that simply hugging your partner for 20 seconds can reduce your stress levels.[42] I personally recommend you skip the countdown and keep on hugging until relaxation washes over you. When my children are stressed and willing to accept a hug from me, I always keep holding on for the moment when they fully exhale and release all their tension.

In a fascinating Japanese study, they found **that talking to someone remotely while hugging a human-shaped cushion, reduced stress levels more than just talking on the phone.**[43] So, the next time stress knocks at your door, and you don't have a willing partner, reach for a pillow, cushion or yoga bolster and embrace the soothing power of hugging it out.

Meditation—The Stress Buffer

A study involving college students concluded that meditation-based practices reduced stress levels and enhanced forgiveness.[44]

Initially, I didn't meditate every day, and consequently didn't notice immediate results. **It was only after consistently meditating for twenty minutes every morning for a couple of weeks, that I began to notice a positive impact on handling daily irritations.**

I've found that the benefits of meditation compound with daily practice.

Think of meditation as a skill, like learning to play the piano. Perhaps at first, you'll just learn the scale. With more practice, you can play a simple nursery rhyme. With further practice you can play a few songs. With thousands of hours you can play any tune after hearing it, and compose your own songs.

The more you meditate, the less time it will take to calm your mind and body.

Another benefit is that often a random intuitive thought will pop into your head during meditation. If it's the solution to a problem I'm having, then I might explore it further—but it is not something I do very often.

For those new to meditation, guided meditation is extremely helpful. It takes the pressure off you and gets you used to relaxing for a set amount of time, to build a habit. As certified meditation teachers, we've included guided meditations for use with this book in the Bonus Content area in Chapter 2: bit.ly/ss-bonus-content

Plug in your headphones, find a comfortable position—sitting or lying down—and listen. **Just ensure it's a safe environment, as you might fall asleep.** If you do fall asleep then that's okay—it's what your body needs right now.

I tend to get a lull in my energy levels around 2-3pm. So, **most days I listen to a 20-minute Yoga Nidra meditation in the afternoon, to come back rested and energized.** There are no poses in Yoga Nidra—it's all about relaxation. It's also known by the more modern name of "Non-sleep deep rest." It guides you through the different layers of your body and mind, using a specific structure. Friends of mine often play a Yoga Nidra meditation after they've eaten lunch, so they can come back refreshed for the second half of the day.

There's an uplifting Yoga Nidra meditation in the Bonus Content section, that will leave you feeling relaxed and with a sense that all is well. **Yoga Nidra reduces stress** and has found to be beneficial for people with PTSD. I personally find it useful when I have squirrelling, anxious thoughts.

If you're venturing into self-guided awareness or mantra meditation, be prepared to face the puppy mind! Many beginners get quickly frustrated and say, "I can't quiet my thoughts."

That's okay, as having a quiet mind is a big misconception. **Gelong Thubten, a Buddhist monk for over thirty years, says that quieting your thoughts is impossible.** Instead, cultivate awareness of the thoughts streaming past your mind, and keep redirecting your focus to a point of concentration, such as your breath, or another part of your body. Whatever works best for you.

Picture your thoughts as a playful, cute puppy. You have one hand on a sturdy stick in the ground—your breath. The other hand is holding the puppy's leash. While you are focusing on the stick, you can see the puppy rolling around and being cute, creating positive thoughts; or growling at things, creating negative thoughts. While you're still relaxed and holding onto the stick, you can see the puppy's movements out the corner of your eye, but it doesn't bother you as you're still looking at the stick.

After a while, your arms get tired and you accidentally let go of the puppy and the breath stick. The puppy bolts off and it goes crashing around in your mind. You chase your puppy for a while, getting lost in your thoughts. **Eventually you remember the breath stick, and you take the puppy back to it.**

Every time you go back to the stick, give yourself a positive "High five!" for doing a great job. It's important to remain relaxed the entire time, and to see every return to your breath as a win. **Never become frustrated about your busy mind, as it is impossible to stop thoughts.**

Some days I'm keeping a good hold of the stick and only occasionally wandering. Other days, I spend more time chasing my puppy than remembering the stick. But each time, I give myself a "High five!" for remembering to return.

How to meditate: Begin by closing your eyes. If you don't like to close your eyes, then you can follow the Zen Buddhist practice of keeping your eyes half open, while facing a blank wall.

Start with the breath—observe it flowing in and out of your nose without trying to control it. Alternatively, incorporate an ancient Sanskrit mantra like "So hum"—I am that. It's a reminder that we are one with the divine universe. Inhale to "so" and exhale to "hum."

When your mind inevitably wanders, gently guide it back to your breath and the soothing rhythm of "So hum." Of course, you can use any mantra or affirmation you prefer—short is best.

Meditating can be thought of as exercising in the gym—You can consider your thoughts as the weights, coming back to your breath as the repetition, ultimately building the muscle of your mind.

Occasionally I imagine a beautiful beach—where the waves come in and out of the shore in time with my breath. You could imagine a beautiful flower swaying in the wind. Do whatever feels most relaxing to you.

Start with one minute and work up to twenty minutes. I've found that when my mind is coming back to the same worry again and again, that a guided meditation like Yoga Nidra can be more relaxing.

ONE MINDFUL BREATH

If you're struggling with even one minute of awareness meditation, then how about just one mindful breath? Really? I'm not joking. It's still meditation.

I learned this in the book, *Joy on Demand: The Art of Discovering the Happiness Within*, by Chade-Meng Tan.

How to do it: with your eyes open or closed, take a deep breath in through your nose, and as you slowly exhale, relax all the tension from your body. Focus on the air moving in and out of your nostrils or lungs. Give 100% of your focus to that one breath. That's it. **Meditation is finished for the day.** Come back tomorrow and take one mindful breath again. I'm not kidding.

If you'd like to level up, then take two breaths. On the second breath, **hold a smile** as you take a deep breath in and slowly exhale—aim to feel joy. If you can't arouse joy, then remember a joyful memory.

If you want to level up again, then find ways of habitualising it into your daily routine. Rather than aiming to take a breath every time you start something, be very specific. It takes time and repetition to build a habit. Perhaps every time you make yourself a drink, you take one mindful breath. Or every time you stop in traffic on your daily commute. Once you've made that into a habit, then pick another specific event to take a breath.

Before you know it, you'll have done one minute of breaths, spread throughout your day. On top of that, you'll benefit from a sense of calm.

Eventually, you'll realise that sitting down for a 20-minute meditation session is really just a series of one mindful breaths added to another, and another.

LETTING GO OF SUFFERING

Michael Singer, author of *'Untethered Soul: The Journey Beyond Yourself'* recommends we observe and sit with the negative emotions we are experiencing. Understand that these thoughts and feelings are temporary. They will pass.

When a negative thought or emotion comes in reaction to something that has happened, or your thoughts start squirreling about a stressor—**take a moment to relax and release the tension in your body.** Let the thought be there and then release its hold on you.

You could also consider sending love to the place in your body where you feel tension. By doing so, you will create space for natural positive emotions like joy and happiness, to flow through you.

This is a difficult but life changing practice—one that Sarah and I are still working on. I highly recommend exploring Michael Singers books if you want to delve deeper.

YOGIC BREATHWORK

Enter the world of "Pranayama," a technique viewed as the expansion of your life force, with roots spanning back over 4,000 years of yogic tradition.

Among the multitude of pranayama techniques, let's explore "Bhramaree" or Bumblebee breath. Yogis have known for thousands of years that this technique can relax the mind and body. It's even thought to raise your vibration and the vibration of those around you.

Bumblebee breath works by signalling our parasympathetic nervous system to calm the body down.

In a study of individuals grappling with stress, depression, anxiety and poor sleep, they found that practicing Bumblebee breath for 15 days resulted in a profound improvement in their symptoms.[45]

How to do it: in essence, sit upright with your back off the chair, then, with a relaxed jaw and closed mouth, release a sustained hum on an exhale. The combination of the vibration, sound, and a prolonged exhale works wonders in calming your system. As certified yogic breathwork teachers, **we've included a Bumble Bee breath tutorial in the Bonus Content area of Chapter 2**, complete with subtle alternatives for discreet practice in public: bit.ly/ss-bonus-content

A word of caution: This technique isn't suitable if you're pregnant, have epilepsy, undergoing any neck, ear, eyes, or head surgery or infections. However, fear not, the tutorial includes alternative practices without vibration, and shorter breath holds for such cases.

Feel free to embrace the Bumblebee breath anytime, including while sitting in traffic jams.

GAMING THERAPY

Jane McGonigal, PhD, author of *'SuperBetter: A Revolutionary Approach to Getting Stronger, Happier, Braver and More Resilient'* **discovered that playing just 10 minutes of Candy Crush Saga, Tetris, or Bejeweled, can help overwrite negative images in your mind.**

It has proven beneficial in research on PTSD, and can help with addiction and other situations where you repeat the same negative visuals in your mind.

How does it work? The visual swapping of objects in the game occupies the visual processing centre in your brain, making it difficult to persist in other thoughts. **The benefits can last as long as 3 to 4 hours.**

WHAT IF...

My mind is hard-wired to look for the worst outcome in any situation. For instance, when I had a really sore throat my mind said: "it's cancer...you're gonna die!"

I now use a technique called "What if..."

When I catch myself thinking negative thoughts, I say out loud a number of positive "what if "statements like: What if it was easy? What if it's nothing? I come up with as many different "what if's," as it takes to make me feel better. Sarah also prompts me when she notices I'm focusing on the worst-case scenarios.

If you want to learn more about this technique, I recommend:

What If It All Goes Right?: Creating a New World of Peace, Prosperity & Possibility—by Mendhi Audlin

Conclusion: Stress Relieving Tools

The journey to reduce overwhelm and stress is a transformative one that requires commitment to regular daily practice.

As we explored the tools in this chapter, we uncovered the power of expressing your thoughts through journaling, talking with people close to you, and also the soothing embrace of a hug.

Breaking the stress cycle involves engaging in physical activity to stay ahead of the avalanche.

But it doesn't stop there. Meditation, with its ability to expand the window of tolerance to stress, becomes a daily practice that compounds over time. Letting go of suffering is a profound shift in perspective, allowing the release of negative emotions to make room for joy and happiness.

Yogic breathwork, such as the Bumblebee breath, serves as ancient secret weapon against stress, supported by modern studies.

Ten minutes of Candy Crush Saga can temporarily overwrite repeated negative thoughts.

And we've learned about the power of asking "What if…," when your mind is only focusing on the worst that could happen.

As we navigate the complexities of modern life, these tools provide an integrated approach to reclaiming bliss, amid chaos.

So, take a deep breath, exhale, embrace these practices, and step into a life where stress is a manageable challenge, not an overwhelming mountain.

CHAPTER 11

And Then What? Finding Fulfilment

As you navigate through this book and make strides to simplify your life, you're inevitably creating space and dialling down your stress to manageable levels. Trim down the number of projects on your plate. Take your time.

Then the key question arises, "And then what?"

Resist the urge to hastily jump into something new. Whatever you contemplate, project yourself mentally into the future. Does it evoke positive feelings…or exhaustion and dread?

As discussed in the money segment in Chapter 5, Tony Robbins' *6 Human Needs* sheds light on **3 needs that yield the most fulfilment and joy: they are love and connection, growth, and contribution.**

LOVE AND CONNECTION

Drawing insights from Chapter 7 on relationships, **consider how to nurture uplifting connections, by intentionally crafting your circle of friends.** This is a process we went through ourselves and was also echoed in the interview with International Opera Singer Deanna Breiwick.

Engage with communities that share your beliefs and passions. Consider getting a loving pet. Remember, it's not about quantity or the number of friends you have on social media, it's the depth of genuine friendships that truly matters.

Growth

Identify your passions. **How can you cultivate these interests and skills?** Invest in books, enrol in courses, attend exhibitions, or seek mentorship. Maybe try experiences slightly beyond your comfort zone, that can propel you to the next level.

Contribution

While you can donate money, you might find more satisfaction in volunteering for a charity that resonates with you—where you witness the direct impact of your efforts.

Taking care of your family is also a form of contribution, a service in its own right.

Is there a business or job that can genuinely benefit people or the planet?

Do you possess helpful knowledge that you're eager to share with others—perhaps your way of contributing to saving the world? It's acceptable if it generates income—after all, everyone has bills to pay.

Spirituality

From the lessons of centenarians in the Blue Zones discussed in Chapter 9, embracing some form of faith practice can potentially extend your life.

If the idea of attending church and worshiping a god doesn't resonate, explore practices like Buddhism and Yoga philosophy, which emphasize self-realization and attaining freedom from suffering. Seek out a community to join.

Conclusion: Finding Fulfilment

As you embark on the journey of simplifying your life and creating space for something more meaningful, it's crucial to ask yourself, "And then what?"

The answer lies in focusing on love and connection, growth, contribution, and spirituality.

By intentionally nurturing uplifting relationships, crafting a supportive social circle, and engaging with communities that resonate with your passions, you lay the foundation for a life rich in love and connection.

Identifying your passions and investing in personal growth through books, courses, and new experiences, propels you toward a more fulfilling existence.

Moreover, contributing to others, whether through volunteering, donating to a meaningful cause, or sharing valuable knowledge to benefit humanity, adds a profound sense of purpose to your journey.

Lastly, don't underestimate the role of spirituality in enhancing your life—and possibly extending it. While it can involve traditional practices like attending church—exploring alternative paths such as Buddhism or Yoga philosophy can lead to self-realization and freedom from suffering. Seek a spiritual community that aligns with your beliefs, and becomes a source of support on your path to a more meaningful and fulfilling life.

In the end, the pursuit of stress reduction through simplicity is not just about eliminating, but about creating the space and opportunity for a life filled with joy and wellbeing.

Thank You for Your Service

If you've read this far in the book, then great job! You may be thinking "OMG I have a million things to simplify Sarah and George…where do I start?"

Don't panic. Make a basic plan. Do one small task on each of your domino goals from your *Domino Action Plan* each day.

When we take the steps to simplify and delete something from our life that is not serving us anymore, it's good to express gratitude for it.

Marie Kondo, author of *The Life-Changing Magic of Tidying Up,* believes everything has a soul. By thanking the object for its service, you can release it without guilt.

Also consider the profound impact your journey towards simplicity can have on others. Join the simplicity movement. Nearly every person I've spoken with wanted to simplify their life. Your unique experiences hold immense value, and by sharing your thoughts in an Amazon review, you contribute to a collective movement to simple living.

Join the conversation, be part of the inspiration, and let your review serve as a testament to the positive change simplicity has brought to your life.

Thank you for being a valuable part of this transformative experience. Here's to the power of your words and the beauty of a life simplified!

Simplicity Secret: How to Reduce Overwhelm and Stress, Make More Money, Improve Your Health and Fitness, and Be Happier

With love, Sarah & George Choy
sarahandgeorge.co.uk

P.S. Remember to download all the goodies from the Bonus Content area:
bit.ly/ss-bonus-content

STEALTH MILLIONAIRE shows you how to easily manage your money like a millionaire and become financially free — so you never need to work again.

Sarah and George went from being in bad debt, to owning a multi-million property portfolio, and became Financially Free by the time Sarah was 39. They quit their jobs to spend time with their family, travelling and pursuing their passions.

Based on real life experience, plus one-to-one interviews with millionaires, they have created a simple blueprint that anyone can use to become financially free.

Who This Book Is For:

- People who don't want to work another 20-30 years

- People who are worried that their pension won't be enough

- People who want to be smarter with their money

Buy Stealth Millionaire today and start your path to great wealth and becoming financially free.
bit.ly/stealthbook

If you've ever been dissatisfied with your job, felt unfulfilled, unmotivated, or might be going through a mid-life crisis, then FIND YOUR PURPOSE will help you to become happier, more fulfilled and live your dream life.

After leaving my career, I felt lost. I didn't know what to do. I didn't know who I was any more. I didn't know which direction to take and I felt like I'd lost my identity. I wrote this book to help me work through the process of regaining my purpose and help others do the same.

Find Your Purpose is an easy to follow, step-by-step guide to take you directly to your purpose in life. As you go through the exercises in this book, you'll be introduced to the variables in the Purpose Formula and learn how to apply them to your life. You'll also gain a new understanding of nearly every life decision you've ever made.

By the end of this book, you'll discover the optimum Purpose that brings you the most joy, happiness, bliss and fulfilment in life. You'll also learn how to get paid for living a life you love.

Buy Find Your Purpose: A Practical Guide for Discovering Your Purpose and Creating a Life You Love bit.ly/fypurpose

REFERENCES

[1] McManus S, Bebbington P, Jenkins R, Brugha T. (eds.) (2016). Mental health and wellbeing in England: Adult psychiatric morbidity survey 2014.

[2] Danziger, S., Levav, J., & Avnaim-Pesso, L. (2011). Extraneous factors in judicial decisions.Proceedings of the National Academy of Sciences,108(17), 6889-6892.

[3] Savings statistics: Average savings in the UK in 2023. Analysis conducted by finder.com

[4] Tiger 21

[5] Fidelity® Millionaire Outlook 2012

[6] Source: officialdata.org stock market returns between 1989 and 2023 excluding inflation.

[7] Source: Calculations by author via annual Compound Interest Calculator on Investor.gov

[8] CNBC: New report finds almost 80% of active fund managers are falling behind the major indexes

[9] US Work Wellbeing 2023 Report: Indeed

[10] Frey, Bruno & Stutzer, Alois. (2008). Stress That Doesn't Pay: The Commuting Paradox. Scandinavian Journal of Economics. 110. 339-366. 10.1111/j.1467-9442.2008.00542.x.

[11] Uncapher MR, Wagner AD. Minds and brains of media multitaskers: Current findings and future directions. Proc Natl Acad Sci U S A. 2018 Oct 2;115(40):9889-9896. doi: 10.1073/pnas.1611612115. PMID: 30275312; PMCID: PMC6176627.

[12] Iyengar, S. S., & Lepper, M. R. (2000). When choice is demotivating: Can one desire too much of a good thing? Journal of Personality and Social Psychology, 79(6), 995–1006

[13] Saxbe, D. E., & Repetti, R. (2010). No Place Like Home: Home Tours Correlate With Daily Patterns of Mood and Cortisol. Personality and Social Psychology Bulletin, 36(1), 71-81. https://doi.org/10.1177/0146167209352864

[14] Lenders C, Gorman K, Milch H, Decker A, Harvey N, Stanfield L, Lim-Miller A, Salge-Blake J, Judd L, Levine S. A novel nutrition medicine education model: the Boston University experience. Adv Nutr. 2013 Jan 1;4(1):1-7. doi: 10.3945/an.112.002766. PMID: 23319117; PMCID: PMC3648731.

[15] Murray, Christopher & Abraham, Jerry & Ali, Mohammed & Alvarado, Miriam & Atkinson, Charles & Baddour, Larry & Bartels, David & Benjamin, Emelia & Bhalla, Kavi & Birbeck, Gretchen & Bolliger, Ian & Burstein, Roy & Carnahan, Emily & Chen, Honglei & Chou, David & Chugh, Sumeet & Cohen, Aaron & Matthay, Ellicott & Cooper, Leslie & Lopez, Alan. (2013). The State of US Health, 1990-2010: Burden of Diseases, Injuries, and Risk Factors. JAMA The

Journal of the American Medical Association. 310. 591-608. 10.1001/jama.2013.13805.

[16] Harris, James & Milton, Nathaniel. (2010). Cholesterol in Alzheimer's Disease and other Amyloidogenic Disorders. Sub-cellular biochemistry. 51. 47-75. 10.1007/978-90-481-8622-8_2.

[17] Ornish D, Scherwitz LW, Doody RS, Kesten D, McLanahan SM, Brown SE, DePuey E, Sonnemaker R, Haynes C, Lester J, McAllister GK, Hall RJ, Burdine JA, Gotto AM Jr. Effects of stress management training and dietary changes in treating ischemic heart disease. JAMA. 1983 Jan 7;249(1):54-9. PMID: 6336794.

[18] Ford ES, Bergmann MM, Kröger J, Schienkiewitz A, Weikert C, Boeing H. Healthy living is the best revenge: findings from the European Prospective Investigation Into Cancer and Nutrition-Potsdam study. Arch Intern Med. 2009 Aug 10;169(15):1355-62. doi: 10.1001/archinternmed.2009.237. PMID: 19667296.

[19] Wolever TM, Jenkins DJ, Ocana AM, Rao VA, Collier GR. Second-meal effect: low-glycemic-index foods eaten at dinner improve subsequent breakfast glycemic response. Am J Clin Nutr. 1988 Oct;48(4):1041-7. doi: 10.1093/ajcn/48.4.1041. PMID: 2844076.

[20] Muraki I, Imamura F, Manson JE, Hu FB, Willett WC, van Dam RM, Sun Q. Fruit consumption and risk of type 2 diabetes: results from three prospective longitudinal cohort studies. BMJ. 2013 Aug 28;347:f5001. doi: 10.1136/bmj.f5001. Erratum in: BMJ. 2013;347:f6935. PMID: 23990623; PMCID: PMC3978819.

[21] Wu QJ, Yang Y, Vogtmann E, Wang J, Han LH, Li HL, Xiang YB. Cruciferous vegetables intake and the risk of colorectal cancer: a meta-analysis of observational studies. Ann Oncol. 2013 Apr;24(4):1079-87. doi: 10.1093/annonc/mds601. Epub 2012 Dec 4. PMID: 23211939; PMCID: PMC3603442.

[22] Singh K, Connors SL, Macklin EA, Smith KD, Fahey JW, Talalay P, Zimmerman AW. Sulforaphane treatment of autism spectrum disorder (ASD). Proc Natl Acad Sci U S A. 2014 Oct 28;111(43):15550-5. doi: 10.1073/pnas.1416940111. Epub 2014 Oct 13. PMID: 25313065; PMCID: PMC4217462.

[23] Joshipura KJ, Hu FB, Manson JE, Stampfer MJ, Rimm EB, Speizer FE, Colditz G, Ascherio A, Rosner B, Spiegelman D, Willett WC. The effect of fruit and vegetable intake on risk for coronary heart disease. Ann Intern Med. 2001 Jun 19;134(12):1106-14. doi: 10.7326/0003-4819-134-12-200106190-00010. PMID: 11412050.

[24] Stanaway, J.D., Afshin, A., Ashbaugh, C. et al. Health effects associated with vegetable consumption: a Burden of Proof study. Nat Med 28, 2066–2074 (2022). https://doi.org/10.1038/s41591-022-01970-5

[25] Rodriguez-Leyva D, Weighell W, Edel AL, LaVallee R, Dibrov E, Pinneker R, Maddaford TG, Ramjiawan B, Aliani M, Guzman R, Pierce GN. Potent

antihypertensive action of dietary flaxseed in hypertensive patients. Hypertension. 2013 Dec;62(6):1081-9. doi: 10.1161/HYPERTENSIONAHA.113.02094. Epub 2013 Oct 14. PMID: 24126178.

[26] Parikh M, Maddaford TG, Austria JA, Aliani M, Netticadan T, Pierce GN. Dietary Flaxseed as a Strategy for Improving Human Health. Nutrients. 2019 May 25;11(5):1171. doi: 10.3390/nu11051171. PMID: 31130604; PMCID: PMC6567199.

[27] Kelly JH Jr, Sabaté J. Nuts and coronary heart disease: an epidemiological perspective. Br J Nutr. 2006 Nov;96 Suppl 2:S61-7. doi: 10.1017/bjn20061865. Erratum in: Br J Nutr. 2008 Feb;99(2):447-8. PMID: 17125535.

[28] Wu H, Flint AJ, Qi Q, van Dam RM, Sampson LA, Rimm EB, Holmes MD, Willett WC, Hu FB, Sun Q. Association between dietary whole grain intake and risk of mortality: two large prospective studies in US men and women. JAMA Intern Med. 2015 Mar;175(3):373-84. doi: 10.1001/jamainternmed.2014.6283. PMID: 25559238; PMCID: PMC4429593.

[29] Wadhawan M, Anand AC. Coffee and Liver Disease. J Clin Exp Hepatol. 2016 Mar;6(1):40-6. doi: 10.1016/j.jceh.2016.02.003. Epub 2016 Feb 27. PMID: 27194895; PMCID: PMC4862107.

[30] Willems MET, Şahin MA, Cook MD. Matcha Green Tea Drinks Enhance Fat Oxidation During Brisk Walking in Females. Int J Sport Nutr Exerc Metab. 2018 Sep 1;28(5):536-541. doi: 10.1123/ijsnem.2017-0237. Epub 2018 Jun 19. PMID: 29345213.

[31] Jalalyazdi M, Ramezani J, Izadi-Moud A, Madani-Sani F, Shahlaei S, Ghiasi SS. Effect of hibiscus sabdariffa on blood pressure in patients with stage 1 hypertension. J Adv Pharm Technol Res. 2019 Jul-Sep;10(3):107-111. doi: 10.4103/japtr.JAPTR_402_18. PMID: 31334091; PMCID: PMC6621350.

[32] Samitz G, Egger M, Zwahlen M. Domains of physical activity and all-cause mortality: systematic review and dose-response meta-analysis of cohort studies. Int J Epidemiol. 2011 Oct;40(5):1382-400. doi: 10.1093/ije/dyr112. Epub 2011 Sep 5. PMID: 22039197.

[33] Woodcock J, Franco OH, Orsini N, Roberts I. Non-vigorous physical activity and all-cause mortality: systematic review and meta-analysis of cohort studies. Int J Epidemiol. 2011 Feb;40(1):121-38. doi: 10.1093/ije/dyq104. Epub 2010 Jul 14. PMID: 20630992.

[34] Hill PL, Turiano NA. Purpose in life as a predictor of mortality across adulthood. Psychol Sci. 2014 Jul;25(7):1482-6. doi: 10.1177/0956797614531799. Epub 2014 May 8. PMID: 24815612; PMCID: PMC4224996.

[35] Musick MA, House JS, Williams DR. Attendance at religious services and mortality in a national sample. J Health Soc Behav. 2004 Jun;45(2):198-213. doi: 10.1177/002214650404500206. PMID: 15305760.

[36] Hong, Joanna & Nakamura, Julia & Berkman, Lisa & Chen, Frances & Shiba, Koichiro & Chen, Ying & Kim, Eric & VanderWeele, Tyler. (2023). Are loneliness and social isolation equal threats to health and well-being? An outcome-

wide longitudinal approach. SSM - Population Health. 23. 101459. 10.1016/j.ssmph.2023.101459.

[37] Vartanian, L. R., Kernan, K. M., & Wansink, B. (2017). Clutter, Chaos, and Overconsumption: The Role of Mind-Set in Stressful and Chaotic Food Environments. Environment and Behavior, 49(2), 215-223. https://doi.org/10.1177/0013916516628178

[38] Walston JD. Sarcopenia in older adults. Curr Opin Rheumatol. 2012 Nov;24(6):623-7. doi: 10.1097/BOR.0b013e328358d59b. PMID: 22955023; PMCID: PMC4066461.

[39] Jaitovich A, Khan MMHS, Itty R, Chieng HC, Dumas CL, Nadendla P, Fantauzzi JP, Yucel RM, Feustel PJ, Judson MA. ICU Admission Muscle and Fat Mass, Survival, and Disability at Discharge: A Prospective Cohort Study. Chest. 2019 Feb;155(2):322-330. doi: 10.1016/j.chest.2018.10.023. Epub 2018 Oct 28. PMID: 30392790; PMCID: PMC6363817.

[40] Nedeltcheva, Arlet & Kilkus, Jennifer & Imperial, Jacqueline & Schoeller, Dale & Penev, Plamen. (2010). Insufficient Sleep Undermines Dietary Efforts to Reduce Adiposity. Annals of internal medicine. 153. 435-41. 10.1059/0003-4819-153-7-201010050-00006.

[41] Drake C, Roehrs T, Shambroom J, Roth T. Caffeine effects on sleep taken 0, 3, or 6 hours before going to bed. J Clin Sleep Med. 2013 Nov 15;9(11):1195-200. doi: 10.5664/jcsm.3170. PMID: 24235903; PMCID: PMC3805807.

[42] Grewen KM, Anderson BJ, Girdler SS, Light KC. Warm partner contact is related to lower cardiovascular reactivity. Behav Med. 2003 Fall;29(3):123-30. doi: 10.1080/08964280309596065. PMID: 15206831.

[43] Sumioka H, Nakae A, Kanai R, Ishiguro H. Huggable communication medium decreases cortisol levels. Sci Rep. 2013 Oct 23;3:3034. doi: 10.1038/srep03034. PMID: 24150186; PMCID: PMC3805974.

[44] Oman D, Shapiro SL, Thoresen CE, Plante TG, Flinders T. Meditation lowers stress and supports forgiveness among college students: a randomized controlled trial. J Am Coll Health. 2008 Mar-Apr;56(5):569-78. doi: 10.3200/JACH.56.5.569-578. PMID: 18400671.

[45] Jagadeesan T, R A, R K, Jain T, Allu AR, Selvi G T, Maveeran M, Kuppusamy M. Effect of Bhramari Pranayama intervention on stress, anxiety, depression and sleep quality among COVID 19 patients in home isolation. J Ayurveda Integr Med. 2022 Jul-Sep;13(3):100596. doi: 10.1016/j.jaim.2022.100596. Epub 2022 Jun 6. PMID: 35693195; PMCID: PMC9167919.

Printed in Great Britain
by Amazon